The Mind–Brain Relationship

The Mind–Brain Relationship

By Regina Pally

in collaboration with David Olds .

Foreword by Mark Solms

International Journal of Psychoanalysis Key Papers Series
Series Editor: Paul Williams

London & New York
KARNAC BOOKS

First published in 2000 by
H. Karnac (Books) Ltd., 58 Gloucester Road, London SW7 4QY
A subsidiary of Other Press LLC, New York.

British Library Cataloguing in Publication Data.

A C.I.P. for this book is available from the British Library.

ISBN 1 892746 68 9

Edited, designed and produced by Sophie Leighton for the *International Journal
of Psychoanalysis*; cover design by Terry Berkowitz.

Printed in Albany, NY, by Boyd Printing Company.

www.karnacbooks.com

CONTENTS

Series Preface   i

Foreword by Mark Solms   iii

Introduction by Regina Pally   v

1: How brain development is shaped by genetic and environmental factors   1

2: How the brain actively constructs perceptions   19

3: Memory: brain systems that link past, present and future   43

4: Emotional processing—the mind-body connection   73

5: Bilaterality: hemispheric specialisation and integration   105

6: Consciousness: a neuroscience perspective (with David Olds)   137

Index   183

SERIES PREFACE
THE INTERNATIONAL JOURNAL OF PSYCHOANALYSIS KEY PAPERS SERIES

This series brings together the most important psychoanalytic papers in the *Journal*'s eighty-year history, in a series of accessible monographs, of which this is the first. The idea behind the series is to approach the *IJP*'s intellectual resource from a variety of perspectives in order to highlight important domains of psychoanalytic enquiry. It is hoped that these volumes will be of interest to psychoanalysts, students of the discipline and, in particular, to those who work and write from an interdisciplinary standpoint. The ways in which the papers in the monographs are grouped will vary: for example, a number of 'themed' monographs will take as their subject important psychoanalytic topics, while others will stress interdisciplinary links (between neuroscience, anthropology, philosophy etc. and psychoanalysis). Still others will contain review essays on, for example, film and psychoanalysis, art and psychoanalysis and the worldwide *IJP* Internet Discussion Group, which debates important papers before they appear in the printed journal (cf. www.ijpa.org). The aim of all the monographs is to provide the reader with a substantive contribution of the highest quality that reflects the principal concerns of contemporary psychoanalysts and those with whom they are in dialogue. We hope you will find the monographs rewarding and pleasurable to read.

Paul Williams,
London, 2000.

FOREWORD

This accessible review by Regina Pally of aspects of the neuroscience literature relevant to psychoanalysts performs an immensely valuable service. The explosion of knowledge in this area over the past few decades makes it almost impossible for the uninitiated psychoanalytic reader to find his or her bearings in it. And yet find their bearings they must, for there is little doubt that the scientific study and treatment of mental disorders (indeed our understanding of the human mind in general) in the twenty-first century will proceed from the fundamental insights that recent neuroscience has generated. Psychoanalysts who fail to assimilate the new knowledge will be increasingly marginalised both scientifically and professionally, and will be unable to participate in this important intellectual revolution.

The first chapter of this book describes how neural circuitry develops epigenetically, in a manner that directly reflects early environmental influences. These experience-dependent circuits might literally be described as the fabric of the ego. The second chapter reviews perceptual mechanisms, emphasising 'top-down' influences (i.e. the impact of memory, motivation, emotion and attentional factors on current perceptual processing). Pally's review of these mechanisms seems to provide a basis for new insights into a host of clinical phenomena (e.g. transference, projection, hallucination) that have played an important part in the development of psychoanalytic models of the mind. The third chapter discusses the structure and function of memory. Few topics are of more importance for psychoanalytic practice than an understanding of the varieties and vagaries of human memory. The contemporary models surveyed by

Pally demonstrate the ongoing fertility of Freud's conception of the dynamic properties and 'constructed' quality of memory. The fourth chapter concerns emotion. Pally correctly emphasises the 'embodied' basis of emotional processing, and draws attention to the unconscious basis and deep evolutionary roots of our emotions, conceptualised by Freud as 'reproductions of very early, perhaps even pre-individual, experiences of vital importance' (1926, *Inhibitions, Symptoms and Anxiety, S.E.* 20, p. 133). The fifth chapter deals with the perennially fascinating topic of hemispheric asymmetry. Pally provides an introductory overview of right/left differences and describes some of the striking phenomena revealed by split-brain studies. She also offers some speculations on the possible implications for psychoanalysis of the bicameral organisation of the forebrain. The sixth and final chapter addresses the fashionable topic of consciousness, the 'final frontier' of neuroscience. This last chapter provides a systematic and comprehensive overview of the state of the art in the field. Here we see how deeply engaged contemporary neuroscience is—no less than psychoanalytic metapsychology—with its philosophical underpinnings.

This book makes it possible for the non-specialist reader to grasp—almost in a single sitting—the main thrust of contemporary brain research on a range of topics of vital interest to psychoanalysis. Readers are bound to want to learn more about one or another of these topics, and in this way, they will be effortlessly inducted into this exciting new era of exploration and discovery in mental science.

Mark Solms,
London, 2000.

INTRODUCTION

This collection of articles appeared as a series in the *International Journal of Psychoanalysis*. My purpose in writing these is to provide psychoanalysts and psychotherapists with the basic, fundamental scientific concepts of neurobiology that are relevant to clinical work with patients. In each article, whenever possible, I try to point out the clinical implications of the scientific data.

I am a psychiatrist and my practice consists mainly of long-term psychotherapy and psychoanalysis. I began reading about neuroscience in 1995, simply for interest, unrelated to my clinical work. However, it soon became clear that neuroscience has a lot to offer clinical work and I have been studying, teaching and writing about it ever since.

These articles contain a lot of neuroanatomy, physiology and experimental data, and for those unfamiliar with science this may be somewhat daunting. To avoid being overwhelmed, I want to encourage the reader not to get lost in the facts. The usefulness of neuroscience rests not in specific facts but in the main principles they illustrate. As a guide to what the important principles are, I include here a list of a few examples of neuroscience concepts that address important questions psychotherapists and psychoanalysts face regularly in their work: (1) how the past influences the present; (2) why we need to *feel* our feelings; (3) why making the unconscious conscious is therapeutic; (4) why verbalising feelings is therapeutic; (5) why we need other people; (6) how the mind and body are integrated with one another; (7) why we tenaciously hold on to belief systems, and how belief systems influence our perceptions, thoughts and behaviours;

(8) how anything we do 'repeatedly' or experience 'repeatedly' can be incorporated at an unconscious level and contribute to habits, character and our relationships with others; (9) how non-verbal behaviour affects both patient and therapist in the treatment situation.

Since in many ways neuroscience validates our theories, it is tempting to focus primarily on this aspect of neuroscience. I think however our work will benefit more from an approach in which the ideas of neuroscience are viewed as having merit in their own right. What I mean is that the value of neuroscience goes beyond its ability to prove or disprove any particular psychoanalytic or psychotherapeutic theory. Neuroscience has much to teach us about the workings of the mind, and about why people think, feel and behave as they do. My approach then is to use neuroscience as an *additional tool* for understanding patients and helping patients to understand themselves. Perhaps someday in the future we might speak of a 'neuroscience interpretation'.

Acknowledgements. I did not accomplish this task alone. First I want to thank my colleagues Hans Miller, John Schumann, Daniel Siegel and Allan Schore for having nurtured my interest in neuroscience, encouraged my writing and taught me much of what I know. I want to express my gratitude to my editors, Arnold Cooper and David Tuckett, for providing me with the unique opportunity to write this series. I am grateful to David Olds, who collaborated with me on the last article in the series, on the topic of consciousness. And of course my thanks to my husband and children for their patience.

Regina Pally,
Los Angeles, 2000.

1: HOW BRAIN DEVELOPMENT IS SHAPED BY GENETIC AND ENVIRONMENTAL FACTORS

We have entered an era of extraordinary discovery about the human brain. Old notions of dichotomy between mind versus brain, nature versus nurture, have been supplanted by a rich web of synergistic relations between mind and brain, nature and nurture. Specifically, according to modern neuroscience, this means that all mental phenomena are assumed to be the result of biological activity of neuronal circuits in the brain. The development of these circuits relies in part on genetic programmes, but is also heavily dependent on the individual's experiences within the environment.

Recognition of the remarkable degree to which brain development is experience-dependent is a striking example of how neuroscience can be integrated with psychoanalysis. These ideas can be considered to lend support to analytic assumptions that early developmental experiences shape subsequent psychological functioning. The overall aim of this book is to integrate the two fields by providing a schematic overview of neuroscience topics that are relevant to the theory and practice of psychoanalysis. In this way the reader will not only know facts about brain functions, but be able to think conceptually about how these functions operate with one another and how they may inform us about our analytic work.

For some, this way of considering 'The Mind' may be rather foreign and difficult to accept. However, as Olds and Cooper in their recent editorial on the value of neuroscience for psychoanalysis recommend: 'We should at least understand what we are being offered, before deciding whether or not' it is profitable to us (1997, p. 221).

The idea that mental life is derived from biological events in neuronal circuits is the reigning doctrine of neuroscience, and therefore
must be taken as a starting point for understanding the empirical
research based on it. For those who criticise these attempts at integration as 'reductionistic', I want to clarify that the emphasis here is
that mental phenomena are derived from biological activity. There is
no intention to equate the mental with the biological.

I have selected topics that are most readily integrated with
psychoanalysis. In this first chapter I address the experience-dependent nature of brain development. The three subsequent chapters cover perception, memory and emotion, and the two following
chapters address aspects of bilaterality and consciousness. The
concepts build on one another with each subsequent chapter. The
data presented throughout is the result of a compilation of animal
research and human research, including in vivo PET scans and
MRIs and computer models of brain function. Before proceeding to
how brain development is shaped by environmental as well as
genetic influences, some preliminary comments are necessary regarding the unique cellular architecture and the evolutionary history of the human brain.

CELLULAR ARCHITECTURE OF THE BRAIN

The brain consists of approximately 10 billion neurons (10^9) *all
activated at the same time* (Edelman, 1992; Edelman & Tononi, 2000).
Each individual neuron, with its axon and branching dendrites,
makes a synaptic connection with approximately 60,000 to 100,000

other neurons. The total number of synaptic connections is in the range of 10^{27}. The number of possible combinations of synaptic connections is in the range of 10^{million}. This is more than the number of positively charged particles in the known universe! The almost infinite number of potential neuronal configurations provides for the brain's vast information processing capacity.

EVOLUTION OF THE HUMAN BRAIN

The architecture and organisation of the brain is the product of its evolutionary history, which indicates that the human brain has evolved and expanded, while still retaining features of three basic 'evolutionary ancestors', reptiles, lower mammals and primates (MacLean, 1990). As a result of natural selection, 'newer' brain structures, which could 'perform' more adaptive functions, were added on to, and integrated with, more primitive structures. The most primitive part, the brainstem, is responsible for vital functions of physiological survival, such as the sleep/wake cycle, heart rate, respiration and body temperature. In addition to the brainstem, the human brain contains structures that are remnants of 'ancestral' brains. Derived from reptilian ancestors is the striatum, also called the basal ganglia. It is responsible for behavioural motor routines that are unique to the particular species, such as territorial displays. Humans have few of the innate behavioural routines found in reptiles and lower animals. However, in humans, once a particular behaviour is repeated many times, such as riding a bicycle or playing a Mozart concerto, the motor patterns are stored in the basal ganglia and can be activated as automatic motor routines. Derived from lower mammals is the palaeomammalian brain, or limbic system. It is associated with emotion and memory, as well as with uniquely mammalian behaviours such as nursing, parental care, play and the infant distress cry.

The most highly evolved part of the brain is the cortex, or neomammalian brain. The part of the cortex that reaches the greatest degree of development in humans is called the prefrontal cortex. It is the 'executive centre' of the brain, responsible for planning for the future, directed attention to a task, delay of gratification, affect regulation and voluntary control of movement (Damasio, 1994; Fuster, 1996). The 'higher', more advanced prefrontal cortex modulates the emotion, behaviour and body physiology processed by the 'lower', more primitive subcortical regions.

There is a tendency to speak about the brain as if a particular function is localised in a particular brain region. However, the brain operates as a dynamic integrated whole (Edelman, 1989). Even a simple perception, such as seeing a cat, involves circuits that traverse the brainstem, limbic system and prefrontal cortex.

GENETIC INFLUENCES ON BRAIN DEVELOPMENT

One half of the entire genome is dedicated to producing the brain, an organ that constitutes only 2 per cent of our body weight. For the nine months of gestation and for a few months after birth, brain growth and development is largely directed by the genetic code (Scheibel & Conrad, 1993). For example, the process by which cells migrate from the primitive neural tube tissue to their final destination in the foetal brain is under direct genetic influence. Another example is that after cells migrate, they develop temporary connections, which 'hold the place' for the more permanent connections that follow. Abnormalities of cell migration may contribute to the development of schizophrenia. One example, after birth, is the myelin sheath, which permits more rapid conduction of impulses along the axon (Kinney et al., 1988). Primary sensory areas myelinate in the first months of life. The prefrontal cortex, a region of higher cognitive skills, begins myelinating at about 3 months of age and continues into young adulthood!

ENVIRONMENTAL INFLUENCES ON BRAIN DEVELOPMENT

The brain is 'born' prematurely. Therefore much of its development occurs postnatally and for many years afterwards. Despite all the rich anatomical connections created under genetic control, the genome is not sufficient to encode all the details as to which connections ultimately become functionally active. To a startling degree, it is interactions with the environment that stimulate the more precise wiring of neural connections (Scheibel & Conrad, 1993). Illustrations of the experience-dependent nature of brain development exist at every level of brain functioning, from the rapid growth of the brain in early childhood to the subtler modifications that occur throughout the lifespan.

How neural circuits are wired

Neuroscientists believe that the functional unit of mental activity is not the single neuron but a circuit of interconnecting neurons all activated at the same time. Perception, memory, emotion, even thoughts and behaviours, are all the product of activated neural circuits. Interactions with the environment cause neurons to wire into circuits, which are sometimes called neural networks or neural assemblies, terms derived from computer models of brain activity. When the brain is exposed to a new event, external (a face, a word) or internal (emotion, physiological state), a unique pattern of neurons is activated. In order to preserve this configuration, connections must be forged between the neurons, creating a new circuit that acts as a symbol, a representation of something in the outside or 'inside' world. In other words, information from internal and external sources is represented in the brain by complex configurations of interconnected neurons (Edelman, 1989).

Recognition occurs when we encounter something that evokes a neural pattern similar to one already preserved, as demonstrated in primate brains and in computer-based neural network modelling (Edelman, 1992; Grossberg, 1999).[1] If a pattern of neurons 'lights up' when you first see the Mona Lisa, the next time you see it, a similar pattern will light up, giving you the sense of recognition. (This process is often referred to as 'pattern matching'.) Because there is redundancy of brain circuits, it is even more accurate to say

---

[1] For a discussion of the way in which psychoanalysis has tried to integrate some of these ideas about pattern-matching and neural circuitry see Basch, 1988 and Hadley, 1992.

that a number of specific neural circuits underlie a particular brain function (Edelman, 1989). Redundancy is adaptive, because if one circuit becomes damaged, another can take its place. Not only is there more than one circuit per function, but individual neurons participate in many circuits, in the way that pixels in a television screen participate in a number of images.

The process by which most neuroscientists suppose connections between neurons are forged is called 'Hebb's rule', which states that if two neurons tend to be electrically active at the same time they will automatically form a connection (Hebb, 1949). If they are already weakly connected, the synapses between them will become strengthened. With regard to brain development it is a matter of 'use it or lose it'. We are born with an overabundance of neurons and dendrites (Diamond, 1988). In the neonatal period a pruning process begins. As a result of experience-dependent circuit development, the neural paths that are used remain, while those that are not used die off.

The role of re-entry circuits

All localised brain regions are richly connected to other brain regions by interconnecting neurons that form re-entry circuits (Edelman, 1989). These circuits, which also depend on experience-dependent 'Hebbian' strengthening, automatically feed information processed in localised brain regions back and forth to other localised regions. It is known that individual attributes of the environment are processed separately. There are relatively separate brain regions to process environmental features such as colour, contour, motion, sound. Other regions for processing the memory of these stimuli and other regions are specialised for co-ordinated motor responses to these stimuli. Through re-entry the brain co-ordinates the information from these separate stimulus processing regions. For example, information processed in the visual cortex, automatically influences processing in the auditory cortex and vice versa. Thus what you see will influence what you hear and what you hear influence what you see. Edelman emphasises that re-entry is an important component of the brain's ability to accomplish complex cognitive tasks.

Sensitive periods for sensory cortex development

Although it has been most extensively studied within the visual system, it is considered a general principle that for normal perceptual capacity to emerge, the sensory cortex must receive very specific kinds of stimulation within a particular time frame, or 'sensitive period'. *In utero* development provides only an approximate sketch of the wiring of the topographically arranged visual cortex. The more precise wiring requires stimulation from postnatal sensory experiences.

Animal experiments were conducted to illuminate the clinical observation that childhood cataracts, if not treated promptly, can lead to permanent blindness. These effects are limited to a sensitive period in childhood. Cataracts that develop later in life, but are surgically corrected, do not lead to blindness.

For binocular vision to develop in monkeys, the brain must receive stimulation from both eyes, within the first six months of life (Hubel & Wiesel, 1962). (In humans the sensitive period extends over the first several years). Normal binocular vision requires that cells in the 4c layer of area 17 of the visual cortex be segregated into clearly defined bands of columnar cells, a topographical arrangement that reflects the distinct axon terminal inputs from each eye. If one eye is sutured at birth, and unsutured at 6 months of age, there is permanent loss of useful vision in that eye. This is associated with failure of cells to segregate into distinct bands. While at birth, axon terminals from each eye project to this cortical area, as a result of sensory deprivation due to suturing the terminals from the deprived eye retract. Those from the normal stimulated eye grow overabundantly, moving into areas they would normally have relinquished to the now retracted terminals.

Sensitive periods for the prefrontal cortex

Even more relevant for psychoanalysts is the picture that is emerging regarding sensitive periods for emotional development. Using a combination of animal and human studies, Schore (1994) proposes a sensitive period of between approximately six months and one year for the development of circuits in the prefrontal cortex that subserve the capacity to self-regulate high positive affect states. Within the sensitive period, the infant must engage in mutually responsive face-to-face, gaze, vocalisation and smiling interactions with the caretaker. The sensitive period correlates roughly with the same age range in which these encounters reach their peak time duration. During these interactions, the infant experiences intense states of excitement that are modulated by the mother's responsiveness (Stern, 1985). After an extensive review of the relevant neuroscience data, Schore argues that these high arousal states specifically induce the sprouting of dopamine-releasing axon terminals, which grow upwards from their cell bodies located in the midbrain, to sites deep in the prefrontal cortex. The increased release of dopamine into prefrontal areas, in turn promotes a growth spurt of synapses and glial cells in this region. According to Schore, the data indicates that these dopaminergic circuits linking mid-brain with prefrontal cortex are a key element of the maturing ability to self-regulate affect states.

Environmental stimulation over the lifespan

Brain growth in response to environmental stimulation is not limited to early development or to 'sensitive' periods. The work of Diamond (1988) demonstrates that throughout life every part of the nerve cell, from soma to synapse, alters its dimensions in response to environmental stimulation. Providing increased environmental stimulation to infant rats enlarges the cortical neurons, increases the number of dendritic connections, and increases the number of glial support cells, all of which increases the thickness of the rat's cortex. Measurable increases of dendritic growth also occur with young adult and even aged rats, if provided a stimulus-rich environment. Even after brain injury, rats reared in an enriched environment show increased dendritic growth.

She also experimented with *in utero* protein deprivation, known to cause a decrease in the number of dendritic connections. After birth, an enriched environment plus protein supplements are better than protein alone to increase dendrites again. Based on these findings, recommendations were made to a health project in Nairobi. Pregnant women were limiting protein in their diet in the last trimester in order to reduce infant head size at birth. It was advised that, in addition to protein supplements, the small-headed newborns should also receive increased stimulation.

It is just as important to stress that decreased stimulation diminishes a nerve cell's dendritic aborisation. Diamond cautions that the ability of an enriched environment to counteract the atrophy caused by an impoverished environment may wane in infancy. Therefore enrichment programmes, such as Head Start in the US, for underprivileged preschoolers, may already be too late (personal communication).

Learning is an example of how stimulation alters neural growth

Studies using the Aplysia snail have provided dramatic examples of how environmental stimulation leads to learning by causing long-term changes in neuronal growth (Kandel & Hawkins, 1992; Bailey & Chen, 1983). These studies focus on two simple forms of learned response to stimuli—habituation and sensitisation.

In habituation, with repeated stimulation, less response to the same level of stimulation occurs. In the short term, this correlates with a decrease in the amount of neurotransmitter released at the synapse. In the long term there is a pruning back of synapses.

Conversely, in sensitisation, with repeated stimulation, there is more response to the same level of stimulation. This correlates, in the short term, with increased release of neurotransmitters. In the long term, repeated exposure to the stimulation activates genes in the nucleus to transcribe new proteins and stimulate the growth of new synapses. This is an example not only of how the brain grows in response to the environment, but also of how the environment influences the expression of the genome!

Environmental stimulation and increased numbers of neurons

For many years it was thought that the brain does not grow any new cells after birth. Up until now, the standard dogma was that environmental stimulation can only increase the number of neuronal connections and the strength of connections, but not the numbers of neurons. We now know that in the hippocampus (involved in long-term memory) new neurons continue to grow even into adulthood. At first the explanation given as to why this growth may not have been previously identified is that no net increase of cells occurs, because the number of old cells dying off balances the number of new cells emerging. But this explanation was soon proven incorrect, by Kempermann et al. (1997), whose research demonstrates that environmental stimulation can increase the number of neuronal cells in the hippocampus. New cells in the hippocampus of mice reared in a stimulation enriched environment live longer. This yields a net increase in the effective number of neurons present in the hippocampus.

BEYOND THE SINGLE BRAIN

It is a characteristic of mammalian brains that they develop in co-ordinated systems with other brains. Just as neurotransmitters carry the stimulus 'message' across the synapse to activate the adjacent neuron, non-verbal behaviours (and in humans, probably words) cross the gap between one brain to activate another brain.

It is well known that in mammals the mother regulates the body physiology of her infant until the infant brain matures enough to provide self-regulation. Hofer (1996) believes that species-specific separation and reunion behaviours link the infant brain neuromodulatory system with the mother's behaviour. Studying rats, he demonstrates that specific maternal factors regulate specific infant factors. Her body-contact regulates the infant's activity level and temperature. Her milk supply regulates the infant's heart rate. Separation from mother triggers the infant's 'separation distress cry'. The mother responds to the pup's call by retrieval, licking and facilitation of milk ejection. Reunion and proximity to mother terminates the distress cry, thus completing the loop in this control system. He proposes that maternal behaviours modulate the infant's physiology by affecting the neuromodulatory system in the infant's brain. Support for his theory rests on the fact that neuro-modulatory substances, such as benzodiazapines and opiates, can act directly on the infant brain to decrease the distress cry during separation. Using rhesus monkeys, Kalin et al. (1995) provide evidence that reunion behaviours (which in the rhesus monkey involve clinging and a vocalisation called girning) operate not only on the brain of the baby but on the brain of the mother as well. In a series of experiments, infants and mothers were separately injected with naltrexone, an opioid antagonist, and morphine an opioid agonist. Naltrexone-treated animals showed increased reunion behaviour; morphine-treated animals showed decreased reunion behaviour. Presumably with naltrexone, the animals engaged in increased reunion behaviours to increase the level of endogenous opioids.

Conversely, with morphine they presumably had decreased reunion behaviours to down-regulate opioid levels. The implication is that the opioid system, in the brain of mother and infant, mediates affiliative behaviours upon reunion. Because opiates induce a positive affect, it follows that reunion behaviours reinforce the positive emotional state of reunion for each member of the dyad.

IN CONCLUSION

The brain's 'design' strikes a balance between circuit permanence and circuit plasticity. As a rule of thumb, more plasticity exists in cortical circuits where new dendrites can grow and synaptic connections can continue to be made throughout life. For cortical functions such as vocabulary or maths, there is a lot of plasticity. People can continue to learn a number of words for the same concept and a number of solutions to a problem. On the other hand, the subcortical limbic 'emotional' circuits that develop in infancy have less plasticity and therefore may have a long-lasting effect on subsequent psychological development (Diamond, 1988; Schore, 1994).

Such 'conservatism' may seem rather limiting, even 'maladaptive'. However, it is circuit permanence that allows children to form and maintain attachments to their parents over the long period of their development and to seek familiar reliable sources of safety and comfort. As mentioned earlier, through maturation the cortex develops the capacity to modulate emotional responses of the subcortex, a process easily observable as children and adolescents grow.

Throughout this article I have presented concepts on which there is relative agreement among neuroscientists. I would like to end, however, on a speculative note regarding psychoanalysis. Since it is known that consciously attending to and verbalising something can enhance cortical activation, it could theoretically be argued that treatments such as analysis enhance cortical functioning, and take advantage of cortical plasticity, to modulate deeply engrained emotional responses.

REFERENCES

BAILEY, C. H. & CHEN, M. (1983). Morphologic basis of long term habituation and sensitization in Aplysia. *Science*, 220: 91–93.

BASCH, M. (1988). *Understanding Psychotherapy*. New York: Basic Books.

DAMASIO, A. R. (1994). *Descartes' Error*. New York: Putnam.

DIAMOND, M. C. (1988). *Enriching Heredity*. New York: The Free Press.

EDELMAN, G. M. (1989). *The Remembered Present*. New York: Basic Books.

—— (1992). *Bright Air, Brilliant Fire*. New York: Basic Books.

—— & TONONI, G. (2000). *A Universe of Consciousness*. New York: Basic Books.

FUSTER, J. M. (ED.) (1996). Frontal lobe and the cognitive foundation of behavioral action. In *Neurology of Decision Making*. Berlin: Springer-Verlag, pp. 47–61.

GROSSBERG, S. (1999). The link between brain learning, attention and consciousness. *Consciousness & Cognition*, 8: 1–44.

HADLEY, J. (1992). Instincts revisited. *Psychoanal. Inq.*, 12: 396–418.

HEBB, D. O. (1949). *The Organization of Behavior: A Neuropsychological Theory*. New York: Wiley.

HOFER, M. A. (1996). Multiple regulators of ultrasonic vocalization in the infant rat. *Psychoneuroendocrinol.*, 21: 203–217.

HUBEL, D. H. & WIESEL, T. N. (1962). Receptive fields, binocular interaction and functional architecture in the cat's visual cortex. *J. Physiol.*, 206: 419–436.

KALIN, N. H. ET AL. (1995). Opiate systems in mother and infant primates coordinate intimate contact during reunion. *Psychoneuroendocrinol.*, 20: 735–742.

KANDEL, E. R. & HAWKINS, R. D. (1992). The biological basis of learning and individuality. *Scientific American,* 267: 79–86.

KEMPERMANN, G. ET AL. (1997). More hippocampal neurons in adult life, living in an enriched dogma. *Nature,* 386 (3 April): 493.

KINNEY, H. C. ET AL. (1988). Sequence of central nervous system myelination in human infancy. II. Patterns of myelination in autopsied infants. *J. Neuropathol. & Experiment. Neurol.,* 47: 217–234.

MACLEAN, P. D. (1990). *The Triune Brain in Evolution: Role in Paleocerebral Functions.* New York: Plenum Press.

OLDS, D. & COOPER, A. (1997). Dialogue with other sciences: opportunities for mutual gain. *Int. J. Psychoanal.,* 78: 219–225.

SCHEIBEL, A. B. & CONRAD, A. S. (1993). Hippocampal dysgenesis in mutant mouse and schizophrenic man: is there a relationship? *Schizophrenia Bulln.,* 19: 21–33.

SCHORE, A. N. (1994). *Affect Regulation and the Origin of the Self.* Hillsdale, NJ: Lawrence Erlbaum.

STERN, D. (1985). *The Interpersonal World of the Infant.* New York: Basic Books.

2: HOW THE BRAIN ACTIVELY CONSTRUCTS PERCEPTIONS

Although subjectively it seems that we simply 'take in' the world as it exists, each and every perception is in fact actively constructed by the brain from the building blocks of individual sensory cues under the guidance and influence of emotion, motivation and prior experience (Gazzaniga, 1995).

Contrary to popular belief, the brain does not operate like a camera taking in a whole scene, but operates more like a feature detector. The brain detects the individual stimulus features of the environment such as edges, contour, line orientation, colour, form, pitch, volume and movement and processes them in separate regions of the cortex. There is no place in the brain 'where it all comes together' as a whole image. To create a perception, the brain takes the pattern of neuronal activity created by the simultaneous processing of all these individual environmental features and compares it with patterns stored in memory. When a match for the current pattern is found, perception occurs. The vast majority of perception occurs non-consciously. Only for the purpose of consciousness does the brain bind together the separate stimulus cues into coherent objects that pass our awareness in a continuous stream of experience (Edelman, 1992; Crick, 1994).

Despite the fact that each person's brain constructs its own perceptions, the results are not specific to each individual. Generally people arrive at a fairly accurate picture of the external world and there is good consensual agreement between people about what they are perceiving. This is because there are constraints and rules built into the constructive process. Our brains were developed under evolutionary survival pressures for adaptively responding to the environment, and the rules and constraints of construction reflect our survival needs in the average expected environment. If this were not the case, if we could not accurately enough perceive what is 'out there' and not be in enough agreement with others of our species regarding the world, our 'ancestors' would not have survived long enough to pass on this system of perception to us.

Some degree of inaccuracy and variation does exist. Brains can be fooled as to what is occurring in the external world, as illustrated by optical illusions. However, there are even rules and constraints on the ways in which it is fooled that lead to consensually agreed illusions. What may be of particular interest to psychoanalysts is the ways in which motivation, emotion and memory can lead to subjective, personal influences over how perceptions are shaped.

The system of perception described here illustrates that perceptual processing contains both ubiquitous, species-wide elements and personal, individual elements. Neuroscience offers psychoanalysis the opportunity for a deeper understanding of how our perceptions are shaped by the past, by our emotions and by influences of which we are unaware.

THE PROCESSING HIERARCHY

The perceptual processing system is organised hierarchically. This refers to how the flow of sensory information begins with the sensory end organ (e.g. retina) and moves along a designated anatomical path to the thalamus, then the sensory cortices and finally the parietal, temporal and frontal association cortices. Simple environmental features are processed lower in the hierarchy. Further along in the hierarchy these simple features are co-ordinated into more complex features. Perception is built up from contributions at all levels of the processing hierarchy (Crick, 1994).

My comments primarily concern visual perception, since most research on perception involves the visual system. However, neuroscientists assume that similar processes also exist for the other sensory modalities (Zeki, 1992; Crick, 1994; Van Essen & DeYoe, 1995).

Visual processing begins at the retina, where photoreceptors process edges by responding to changes in light intensity. The retina projects to the lateral geniculate nucleus of the thalamus and then to the striate visual cortex, also called V1. Neurons in V1 pro-cess line orientation, line length and form. V1 projects to the extrastriate visual cortex, which includes V2, 3, 4 and 5. Cells in V3 process dynamic form, the shape of objects in motion. Cells in V5 process motion. Cells in V4 process colour. Damage to V4 causes achromatopsia, the selective loss of colour perception. Form remains intact, but a Matisse will be seen without the vibrant colours.

At this level of processing, neurons tend to have a preferred stimulus to which they are maximally responsive. Neurons 'interested' in line orientation will respond more to one particular angle, such as 30 degrees, or perhaps 45 degrees (Le Vay et al., 1975; Crick, 1994). Cells preferring colour will have a preferential wavelength to which they respond. Cells sensitive to motion will be maximally responsive to a particular velocity, others to a particular direction of motion. Responsiveness of cortical sensory cells is graded, with more activation the more a feature resembles that cell's preference and less activation the less the feature resembles the cell's preference (Calvin, 1996). The resulting representation of a feature involves the graded responses of large populations of cortical neurons all with similar 'interest'.

Cells in the visual cortex project to the parietal and temporal cortex, where cells are less 'fussy' and respond to a broader range of stimulus features. The inferior temporal cortex processes the complex features important to identifying objects. The posterior parietal area processes the complex stimulus cues that relate to spatial location, spatial relationships and depth perception. At the level of the prefrontal cortex, the temporal 'what' information and the parietal 'where' information is finally integrated (Rao et al., 1997).

Up until now I have focused on processing of inanimate environmental features. The cells that process environmental features such as social signals are located in the temporal cortex, orbitofrontal cortex, as well as a sub-cortical structure known as the amygdala (Brothers, 1992). Social signals are those facial expressions, gestures and vocalisations that animals use to communicate their emotions, intentions and state of mind to one another. As with the sensory cortex, some degree of feature preference exists. For example, some cells are especially responsive to frontal views of faces, others to faces in profile, still others to arched eyebrows, bared teeth, or direct eye contact. The most recent research with humans reveals that some neurons are especially sensitive to whether a face is male or female and some selectively responsive to which emotion a face is expressing (Fried et al., 1997).

'BOTTOM-UP' PROCESSING

'Bottom-up' processing refers to how individual sensory stimuli activate brain cells and how simple individual features of the environment are co-ordinated with one another and built into more complex features of the environment at a neuronal level. The term 'bottom-up' does not relate to the 'bottom' of the processing hierarchy. It relates to the mechanisms within the anatomical hierarchy as a whole. 'Bottom-up' mechanisms are involuntary, always unconscious and are more closely related to the physical properties of the environmental stimuli and the architectural organisation of the sensory cortex.

Later on I will discuss 'top-down' mechanisms, which pertain to how memory, motivational state, emotion, attention and imagery can shape perceptions. 'Top-down' influences can be voluntary and conscious.

Cortico-cortical connections

The cortex is richly endowed with cortico-cortical dendritic pathways that link neurons in the superficial layers of the cortex (Calvin, 1996). They are sometimes referred to as re-entry circuits (Edelman, 1989). These cortico-cortical connections allow sensory information to flow both ways between regions of the cortex, providing the means by which separate sensory regions can influence one another and separate sensory cues can be integrated with one another.

Neuroscientists hypothesise that cortico-cortical connections are responsible for the optical illusion of visual contours (Crick, 1994). In the Kaniza triangle (Figure 1 below) an observer sees a triangle extending between the 'pac man' like shapes, even though the lines of the triangle do not 'objectively' exist. It is presumed that cells in V1 respond to 'actual' contours and send information via these connections to V2, which exhibits electrical activity corresponding to the 'illusory' contour. All perceptions, even 'inaccurate' ones such as optical illusions, are assumed to correlate with actual neuronal activity.

As a result of cortico-cortical connections, perception can occur even in occluded areas of the visual field. Perception attributed to the occluded area occurs due to 'filling in', because information

Figure 1: Kaniza triangle: illusory contours correspond to brain activity.

about colour, texture or movement can be transmitted from the areas of the visual field that are not occluded (Ramachandran & Gregory, 1991).

Sensory context

Perception is very sensitive to the sensory context in which a stimulus is encountered. This means that a stimulus can be perceived differently depending on what other environmental stimuli are close by.

This is believed to involve cortico-cortical connections in which input from other cortical regions can alter the sensitivity of a cell to its preferred attribute, causing it to fire with different intensity, greater or lesser, than it would have without that input (Gilbert, 1995). Two parallel lines transected by multiple lines of varying angles will appear not to be parallel. Perception of the colour of an object varies according to the colour of adjacent objects.

Polymodal sensory information

Perceptual processing begins with each sensory modality separated. Eventually the various sensory information is integrated, as it moves further along in the hierarchy. While drinking a cup of coffee you are aware simultaneously of the feel of the cup, its appearance and the aroma of the coffee. Polymodal integration probably occurs in parietal and temporal association cortices (Crick, 1994).

How sensory modalities influence one another

Sensory processing in one modality can influence sensory processing in other modalities. A particularly fascinating example occurs between the visual and auditory system. Watching a speaker's lips and lip-reading, in normally hearing individuals, activates the auditory cortex, even in the absence of auditory speech sounds (Calvert et al., 1997). Lip-reading probably augments auditory comprehension during normal spoken conversation under noisy conditions.

How separate features are grouped into objects

Different stimulus features of the same object are processed by cortical neurons in different brain areas. At the same time cortical neurons respond to their preferred stimulus in different objects. How does the brain determine which activity goes with which? Using a cup of coffee as an example, the brain separately processes the edge of the rim, the contour of the handle, the angle of the sides, the white colour of the mug, the texture of the ceramic and the aroma of the coffee. Extraordinary as it may seem, there is no place in the brain that contains a whole image of an object. Each sensory feature is processed in a separate region of the cortex. However, the brain has mechanisms by which it determines which edge goes with which contour, which texture with which surface and which aroma with which cup.

The most currently accepted mechanism for binding together separate features is a process called temporal synchronisation (Singer, 1995; Calvin, 1996). Electrical activity of neurons oscillate at different frequencies. Synchronisation occurs when cells oscillate at the same frequency. Neurons participating in the encoding of related 'contents' get organised through their cortico-cortical connections with the result that eventually their electrical discharges become synchronised. For example, spatially segregated cells (even in different hemispheres!) responding to the same stimulus cue (let's say a line of particular orientation) will show a synchronous pattern of firing (Gray & Singer, 1989; Engel et al., 1991).

Neurons responding to different features (let's say one responds to form, one to movement and one to colour) will exhibit synchronised

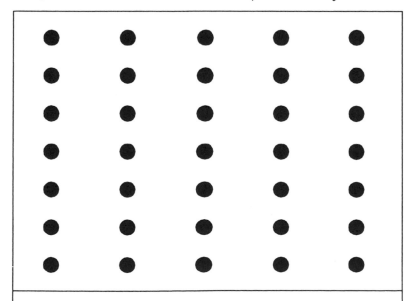

Figure 2: The Gestalt principle of proximity.

firing if they are responding to different features of the same object. Neuroscientists theorise that a special case of synchrony may be involved in contributing to conscious awareness (Crick & Koch, 1990).

Gestalt criteria are 'grouping' tendencies (Finkel & Sajda, 1994). 'Proximity' is the tendency to group together things that are close to one another. In Figure 2 above, the dots are closer together in the vertical than in the horizontal; therefore you see them organised as vertical lines.

Synchronisation of cell activity reflects a number of Gestalt criteria (Singer, 1995). 'Continuation' is the tendency to 'see' two lines that intersect (imagine an X) as two lines instead of four lines meeting at a point. The neurobiological correlate is that cells in diverse locations all responding to different parts of the same continuous

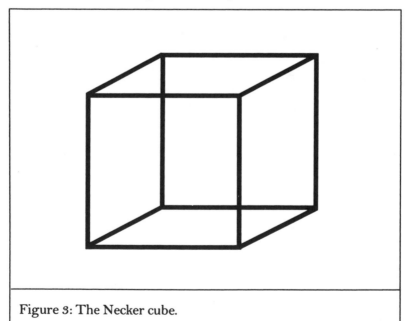

Figure 3: The Necker cube.

contour will synchronise their firing. Therefore, the contour parts are seen as a whole.

'Similarity' is the tendency to group things together that have an obvious visual property in common, such as colour or direction of movement. At the neurobiological level, cells that process spatially separate contours but that are moving in the same direction, will become synchronised. When a cat slinks through the tall grass you still perceive a whole cat. The contours, although partially occluded by the tall grass, all move together and their corresponding neural activity is synchronised.

Competition between inputs from each eye

The input from both eyes is not always completely integrated. The Necker cube (Figure 3 above) illustrates this phenomenon.

The same pattern of lines and angles can be organised into two different perceptions, two cubes each oriented differently, each of which represents the slightly differing input from each eye. If you stare at the figure you will notice that the perception keeps switching between the two objects. Although two possible perceptions can be made from the stimuli, the brain only consciously generates one at a time.

CURRENT PERCEPTION REQUIRES COMPARISONS WITH THE PAST

The separate features of the environment stimulate particular patterns of neuronal activity in the brain. The brain does not perceive the external environment, nor the separate stimulus features. Rather, the brain recognises the patterns of neuronal activation within the brain itself. For perception to occur, the brain searches for a match between the current pattern of neuronal activation, and patterns stored in memory from prior experience (Edelman, 1989, 1992; Kosslyn & Sussman, 1995; Ornstein, 1991). To minimise effort expenditure, the brain does not analyse every detail of a pattern, but makes a quick assessment of just enough details to find a 'good enough match'. When a 'good enough' match is found, perception occurs.

If no match is found, the brain assesses more details of the pattern or consciously pays attention to the situation to seek more information until a match can be found. If still no match is found, a new category of experience is generated, whose pattern is now stored in memory for later pattern-matching. Each category of experience is represented by its own pattern.

The brain automatically and continually processes sensory stimuli, matches patterns and generates perceptions. This is why when you see a cloud you inevitably 'see' objects, fish, boats etc., as your brain automatically generates perceptions from pattern-matching using the sensory cues of the cloud.

'TOP-DOWN' PROCESSING

Memory

Although already mentioned in its own section for the purpose of clarity, memory is the classic example of 'top-down' processing. As discussed previously, patterns of neuronal activity stored in memory are compared with current ones resulting from current sensory stimulation.

Since the brain only requires that the match be 'good enough', current perceptions are strongly biased by previous experiences. Pattern-matching has special relevance for psychoanalysis, particularly transference. If a current situation activates a pattern that is similar to one stored in memory, because the brain only looks for a 'good enough' match the brain may conclude that two different situations are the same. For this reason we tend to 'see' what we have seen before.

Motivational relevance

We are more likely to perceive cues from the environment that are relevant to our current needs than stimuli that are currently irrelevant (Beardsley, 1997). More often a person will notice the aroma from their neighbour's grill if they are hungry than if they have just eaten.

Emotion

Emotions influence how stimuli are interpreted. Fear and anxiety enhance the tendency to interpret stimuli as dangerous (Van der Kolk, 1993). Traumatised patients in a fearful hyper-aroused state may perpetuate that state because their perceptual system is more likely to interpret even seemingly neutral stimuli as frightening.

Attention

What is important to keep in mind is that amount of activity is the key factor in capturing the perceptual system. The patterns with the most activity 'win' (Calvin, 1996). Focused attention on a stimulus enhances the activity in the cells processing that stimulus and not paying attention leads to decreased activity (Moran & Desimone, 1985). When attention enhances activity in a particular group of cells, the pattern of that group is more likely to be the dominant pattern and thus more likely to be what is perceived. Experiments with monkeys using single-cell electrodes in individual cells in the visual cortex show that activity in a particular cell is greatly increased when the monkey is actually paying attention to a particular stimulus as compared to when the stimulus is within the monkey's visual field but not directly attended to. The prefrontal cortex is the most likely candidate for the place in the brain that regulates directed attention (Posner, 1994).

Experiments using human subjects reveal that what you are intentionally looking for has an impact on the activity within the perceptual processing system in a similar way to focused attention in monkeys (Corbetta et al., 1991). Subjects are shown a number of the same moving coloured shapes and asked to discriminate amongst them based on colour, shape or movement. Although the images presented are the same, brain activity is different depending on which attribute is looked for. If asked to look for motion, the greatest activity is in V5. When focusing on colour, the greatest activity is in V4. When shape is sought the greatest activity is in the 'what' region of the temporal pathway. When subjects are asked to study a series of faces flashed on a screen, activity is greater in the 'what' temporal pathway when subjects are asked to decide whether the faces are of the same person or not. The activity is greater in the 'where' parietal pathway when the subjects are asked questions about the location of the faces on the screen.

Similar mechanisms may be involved in trauma. Victims of trauma can direct focused attention to neutral aspects of the situation, such as the ceiling, in order not to perceive painful elements of the experience (Siegel, 1996).

Imagery

Visually imagining a cup of coffee, even with one's eyes closed, activates the same visual cortex as seeing the cup. As a result of shared circuitry, visual imagery can influence visual perception (Kosslyn & Sussman, 1995). It is postulated that input derived from imagery adds electrical activity to sensory details derived from external sources. This speeds up the process as to which pattern captures the perceptual system. Experiments conducted on humans reveal that imagining an object prior to being shown a jumbled-up version of the object enhances the likelihood of recognising what the object is (Rumelhart & McClelland, 1986).

Evidence suggests that processes related to voluntary visual imagery occur routinely, but unconsciously, as facilitators of perception. Neuroscientists assume that when sensory input is insufficient or ambiguous (your pen is lying on the desk partly covered by a journal), input derived from stored images, real or imagined, routinely adds activity to the sensory cortex, providing additional sensory information (albeit from internal sources) to resolve uncertainties and ambiguities in perceptual processing. Thus you can perceive the pen as your Mont Blanc, not just any black pen. The influence of imagery on perception blurs the distinction between fantasy and reality.

THE BRAIN IS SEPARATE BUT INTEGRATED

Although the brain has so many diverse regions, it functions in a remarkably integrated way.

Visual linked with motor

Visual imagery, such as visually imagining writing letters, activates not only the visual cortex but also the motor regions that execute these motor actions (Kosslyn & Koenig, 1992). Visual imagery is even constrained by the same constraints as the physical body (Shepard & Cooper, 1982). It takes longer to mentally rotate an object through more degrees, just as it takes longer to actually rotate that object in the external environment.

The link between visual perception and motor actions may be a bridge to understanding imitation (Kosslyn & Sussman, 1995). What one sees may automatically activate motor programmes (e.g. mirror neurons) related to what one is seeing, which helps explain why observing someone else's behaviour allows one to carry out that behaviour (Rizzolatti & Arbib, 1998).

Object permanence

Object permanence is the knowledge that an object is still present even though it is no longer visible. The link between the visual sensory system and the motor system provides some neurobiological explanations for this psychological capacity (Graziano et al., 1997). When a monkey looks at an object, cells in the visual cortex are activated and, at the same time, cells in the ventral premotor cortex responsible for arm and head movements are also activated. Single electrode readings reveal that the motor cells remain active even after the lights are turned off and the monkey can no longer see the object. Motor cells encode the presence of a visual stimulus that is no longer visible, so the body still 'senses' the presence of the object even if it cannot see the object. These cells may underlie the ability to reach for or avoid objects even in the dark or when the eyes are closed (Rizzolatti et al., 1997).

THE 'CONFLICTED BRAIN'

Perception evolved to facilitate adaptive behaviour. Brains that could most quickly detect food, foes and mates so as to 'decide' what if any behavioural response to initiate would be the most likely to pass on their progeny. However, the pressure for speed of response is balanced against a pressure for accuracy, in order to run from foes not mates and to eat only the berries you know are edible.

As a result of these two survival mandates, speed and accuracy, the brain has a split perceptual system (LeDoux, 1995). One part has the capacity for quick responses that require only the detection of a few simple environmental features before initiating a behaviour. The other slower part responds after more detailed input from many environmental features and therefore is more accurate. In the quick, short route, sensory stimuli pass from the sensory end organ, let's say the retina or cochlea, through the thalamus and directly to the amygdala, which can initiate survival behaviours like running. The quick short route, because it bypasses the cortex, cannot involve conscious awareness. You begin to run before you are consciously aware of the large looming figure heading directly towards you. At the same time, sensory stimuli travel the long, but slower route from the thalamus to the sensory cortex, to the hippocampus and then to the amygdala and orbitofrontal cortex. Now receiving more detailed information, the first 'emergency' response can be inhibited and another behaviour can, if desired, be initiated. There is no need to run because in fact the large looming figure is your neighbour's friendly Great Dane coming up to greet you. Petting would be more appropriate than running. The longer slower system involves the cortex and therefore can include conscious awareness.

ANECDOTAL PERCEPTIONS ILLUSTRATE THESE MECHANISMS

A personal anecdote of mine illustrates how prior experience influences current perception. While cycling through the hospital grounds I passed what appeared to be a very small red barn. I pondered, was it a large dog house for guard dogs? Was it a storage bin? On the return route I took a second look. It was a red garbage dumpster, with its black lid open and angled outwards. But why did my brain at first hypothesise a small barn? A few months later the mystery was solved when I looked up at my wall at a print I have of Georgia O'Keeffe's 'Lake George Barns'. Tucked in amongst the blue barns is a small red one, the same hue as the dumpster and with a roof the same angle as that made by the dumpster's open lid. I assume a neural pattern of this barn was stored in my memory and that the current dumpster activated a pattern that when quickly assessed for just a few details (roof angle and colour) caused my brain to jump to the conclusion that what I was seeing on my bike ride was a barn. When I consciously paid attention to more details another perception arose.

The brain does not know if it is making the wrong interpretation (Ornstein, 1991). Another anecdote illustrates this. Driving my car through a busy intersection I saw a blind man with a 'seeing eye dog' and a cane waiting on the corner, to my left, for the light to change so he could cross. Immediately I felt sorry for him because the intersection was so wide and busy.

As I made a left turn and passed him more closely, I saw he had a 'pooper scooper' not a cane. I wondered what a blind man was doing with a pooper scooper. How could he see to scoop the poop? An instant later, after I had already passed him, the complete perception hit me. He was just a man walking his dog! However, he was wearing dark glasses, staring straight ahead at the light and held the dog's leash at the angle a blind person might hold a 'seeing eye dog' and the scooper had a long handle held out at the angle a blind person might hold a cane. The quick, 'jump to conclusions' perceptual system processed dark glasses, head straight ahead, arm angle,

long stick and 'guessed' this was a blind man. More details, from the
longer slower perceptual route, corrected the perception and I realised it was a sighted man walking his dog. If I had turned right
instead of left at the intersection and not got a second and longer
look I might not have corrected my perception.

Most of the time the brain interprets stimuli correctly enough,
otherwise our ancestors would not have survived to pass on this
system to us. What pressures exist for the perceptual system to
correct significant inaccuracies? We are more likely to use the accu-
racy-enhancing properties of consciousness in situations that matter to us physically and emotionally or situations that are novel or
unexpected (Edelman, 1989, 1992). A blind man crossing the street
is not unusual and would not normally cause me to question my
perception. I just happened to pass nearby and get more details. I
could just as easily have turned right and not given my 'mispercep-
tion' another thought. The barn, however, was unexpected and
caused me to consciously investigate further.

IMPLICATIONS AND CONCLUDING REMARKS

The role of pattern-matching in perception suggests an explanation for people's tendency to repeat painful situations from the past.
The implication is not so much that people in fact repeat the same
experience but that they tend to interpret current situations with a
bias towards what has occurred in the past.

Although consciousness is only a small part of perception, it
serves a crucial function, since it enables the brain to pay more

attention to environmental details, to gather more facts, so to speak, to enhance perceptual accuracy. During novel situations, when no pattern-match is found, consciousness gathers the details so a new pattern can be established and a new category of experience generated. This is commonly seen as children develop. On first encountering an animal they have never seen, such as a racoon, the child may call it 'kitty', because that is a pattern of furry animals that is already stored. Only with conscious focus on details such as the characteristics of the face or the tail might a new category of animal be generated. One way to conceptualise psychoanalysis is as a treatment method that encourages paying conscious attention to the specific details of the interpersonal transference situation in order to develop greater perceptual accuracy and, when necessary, to be able to generate new categories of interpersonal experience.

REFERENCES

BEARDSLEY, R. (1997). The machinery of thought. *Scientific American*, August issue: 78-83.

BROTHERS, L. (1992). Perception of social acts in primates: cognition and neurobiology. *Neurosciences*, 4: 409-414.

CALVERT, C. A. ET AL. (1997). Activation of auditory cortex during silent lip reading. *Science*, 276: 593-595.

CALVIN, W. H. (1996). *The Cerebral Code*. Cambridge, MA: MIT Press.

CORBETTA, M. F. ET AL. (1991). Selective and divided attention during visual discrimination of color, shape and speed: functional anatomy of positron emission tomography. *J. Neurosci.*, 11: 2383–2402.

CRICK, F. (1994). *The Astonishing Hypothesis.* New York: Macmillan.

—— & KOCH, C. (1990). Towards a neurobiological theory of consciousness? *Semin. Neurosci.*, 2: 263–275.

EDELMAN, G. (1989). *The Remembered Present.* New York: Basic Books.

—— (1992). *Bright Air, Brilliant Fire.* New York: Basic Books.

ENGEL, A. K. ET AL. (1991). Interhemispheric synchronization of oscillatory neuronal responses in cat visual cortex. *Science,* 252: 1177–1179.

FINKEL, L. F. & SADJA, P. (1994). Constructing visual perception. *Amer. Scientist,* 82: 224–237.

FRIED, I. ET AL. (1997). Single neuron activity in human hippocampus and amygdala during recognition of faces and objects. *Neuron,* 18: 753–765.

GAZZANIGA, M. S. (ED.) (1995). *The Cognitive Neurosciences.* Cambridge, MA: MIT Press.

GILBERT, C. D. (1995). Dynamic properites of adult visual cortex. In *The Cognitive Neurosciences.* Cambridge, MA: MIT Press, pp. 73–90.

GRAY, C. M. & SINGER, W. (1989). Stimulus-specific neuronal oscillations in orientation columns of cat visual cortex. *Proc. Nat. Acad. Sci. USA,* 86: 1698–1702.

GRAZIANO, M. S. ET AL. (1997). Coding the locations of objects in the dark. *Science,* 277: 239–241.

KOSSLYN, S. M. & KOENIG, O. (1992). *Wet Mind: The New Cognitive Neuroscience.* New York: Free Press.

—— & SUSSMAN, A. L. (1995). Roles of imagery in perception: or, there is no such thing as immaculate perception. In *The Cognitive Neurosciences*. Cambridge, MA: MIT Press, pp. 1035-1042.

LEDOUX, J. (1995). Emotion: clues from the brain. *Ann. Rev. Psychol.*, 46: 209-235.

LE VAY, S. ET AL. (1975). The pattern of ocular dominance columns in macaque visual cortex revealed by a reduced silver stain. *J. Comp. Neurol.*, 159: 559-575.

MORAN, J. & DESIMONE, R. (1985). Selective attention gates visual processing in the extrastriate cortex. *Science*, 229: 782-784.

ORNSTEIN, R. (1991). *The Evolution of Consciousness*. New York: Simon and Schuster.

POSNER, M. (1994). Attention: the mechanisms of consciousness. *Proc. Nat. Acad. Sci.*, 91: 7398–7403.

RAMACHANDRAN, V. S. & GREGORY, T. L. (1991). Perceptual filling in of artificially induced scotomas in human vision. *Nature*, 350: 699-702.

RAO, S. C. ET AL. (1997). Integration of what and where in the primate prefrontal cortex. *Science*, 276: 821-824.

RIZZOLATTI, G. & ARBIB, M. A. (1998). Language within our grasp. *Trends in Neuroscience*, 21: 188–94.

—— ET AL. (1997). The space around us. *Science*, 277: 190-191.

RUMELHART, D. E. & MCCLELLAND, J. L. (EDS)(1986). *Parallel Distributed Processing: Explorations in the Microstructure of Cognition*. Cambridge, MA: MIT Press.

SHEPARD, R. H. & COOPER, L. A. (1982). *Mental Images and Their Transformations*. Cambridge, MA: MIT Press.

SIEGEL, D. J. (1996). Cognition, memory and dissociation. *Child and Adolescent Psychiatric Clinics of North America*, 5: 509-536.

SINGER, W. (1995). Time as coding space in neocortical processing: a hypothesis. In *The Cognitive Neurosciences*. Cambridge, MA: MIT Press, pp. 91-104.

VAN DER KOLK, B. A. (1993). Biological considerations about emotions, trauma, memory and the brain. In *Human Feelings: Explorations in Affect Development and Meaning*. Hillsdale, NJ: Analytic Press, pp. 221-240.

VAN ESSEN, D. C. & DE YOE, E. A. (1995). Concurrent processing in the primate visual cortex. In *The Cognitive Neurosciences*. Cambridge, MA: MIT Press, pp. 383-400.

ZEKI, S. (1992). The visual image in mind and brain. *Scientific American*, 267: 68-76.

3: MEMORY: BRAIN SYSTEMS THAT LINK PAST, PRESENT AND FUTURE

'Memory is the capacity to look from the present to the past and at the same time witness the passing of the present into the future.'

H. J. Markowitsch (1995, p. 767).

INTRODUCTION

There are many kinds of memory. One is the memory for what you did last night. Other types of memory are for how to tie your shoes, or who William the Conqueror was, or how you felt when your grandmother died, or for remembering a seven-digit telephone number while dialling it. All of these are different still from the kind of memory you use when you go back to what you were doing before being interrupted by a telephone call. Memory is the umbrella rubric under which each of these diverse phenomena can be classified. What unites them under the term 'memory' is that all involve the neural representation of information to which a person was previously exposed and which can be reactivated for use in the present (Baddeley, 1995; Schacter, 1995; Shimamura, 1995; Tulving, 1995). Memory is closely allied with learning, whether learning facts, or learning relationships between events; 'when I cry, mommy comes and picks me up' (Alkon, 1992). Memory, then is about the past, but it also helps to anticipate the future. Neuroscientists generally agree that there are a number of kinds of memory, each processed in a different brain system (Schacter & Tulving, 1994). Typically these systems interact, but they can at times operate independently of one another.

The neuroscientific understanding of memory centres on issues related to the unconscious mind, and therefore ought to be of particular interest to psychoanalysts. Research findings support the analytic idea that unconscious material can affect conscious functioning. However, neuroscience does explain this phenomenon differently from psychoanalysis, since neuroscience does not even address the basic psychoanalytic concept that represssion can result in unconscious material. I think the ideas of neuroscience are compatible with analytic approaches, but do challenge analysts to broaden their thinking on this subject.

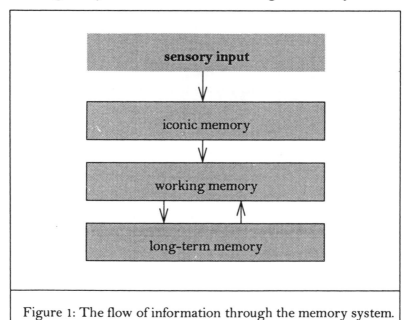

Figure 1: The flow of information through the memory system.

THE FLOW OF INFORMATION THROUGH THE MEMORY SYSTEM

Information flows through the memory system in a series of stages (see Figure 1) (Atkinson & Shiffrin, 1968).

Iconic memory

Iconic memory lasts less than a second (Baddeley, 1995). Iconic memory occurs when external stimuli activate sensory end organs and these areas remain in an active state long enough for the information to be processed and lead to a perception. One example of iconic memory is the visual after-image caused by photochemical changes in the retina.

Working memory

Working memory, also called short-term memory, refers to information that is held for only a few minutes, making possible a brief lingering impression of the individual's world, beyond the duration of the actual physical presence of environmental stimulation (Kupferman, 1991). Information represented neuronally in working memory remains in a labile state, subject to influences that can either disrupt it or strengthen it so it is stored more permanently in long-term memory. Information in working memory can come from the current stimulus situation or be temporarily 'copied' from long-term storage, as for example when trying to recall important figures of World War II.

Working memory is considered to be a temporary, 'erasable work space', able temporarily to hold a number of pieces of relevant information at the same time and manipulate them if necessary. Working memory depends on the prefrontal cortex (Fuster, 1994; Beardsley, 1997). An example of working memory is the capacity immediately to repeat back a sequence of digits such as a telephone number or to hold numbers in your head to add them up when calculating the restaurant tab (Baddeley & Warrington, 1970). Words are held temporarily in working memory when you need to remember the beginning of a sentence in order to make sense of the end of it. The 'delayed choice' test illustrates how working memory helps an animal to deal with a number of pieces of information simultaneously. An animal is taught to point to a 'target' stimulus, a particular location or image. After a brief time-delay during which the target stimulus is not present, the animal is tested. Working memory is intact if the animal can remember the location or image. During the delay, in the absence of the 'target', the cortical neurons processing the 'target' stimulus show reduced firing, while neurons in the prefrontal cortex 'hold' the information. Even if during the delay a monkey is presented with a 'distracting' stimulus, cell firing in the prefrontal cortex can still hold the 'target' while the animal attends to the distracting stimulus (Miller et al., 1993; Beardsley, 1997).

Working memory is responsible for the search and retrieval of information from long-term memory that is involved in many higher cognitive functions. In fact all higher cognitive functions, such as the comprehension of complex information, reasoning, decision-making and planning for the future depend on the ability of working memory to hold a number of pieces of information simultaneously. Intelligence itself may be the result of working memory's ability to 'juggle' many possibilities.

Long-term memory

Long-term memory is the permanent storage of information. Working memory is further processed in order to be encoded and stored permanently (Kupferman, 1991). Information from long-

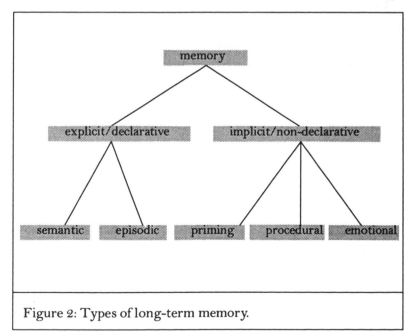

Figure 2: Types of long-term memory.

term storage flows backwards into working memory, for the pur-pose of memory search and retrieval tasks.

Memory deficits can be the result of problems at any one of these stages. Repression, for example, might result from problems with encoding, consolidation or retrieval.

EXPLICIT MEMORY/DECLARATIVE

Long-term memory itself is divided into explicit and implicit memory (Figure 2 above).

Explicit memory, also called declarative memory, is the kind of memory that is revealed by the conscious recollection of pre-vious experience, and generally refers to the memory of specific events and facts (Schachter, 1995; Squire & Knowlton, 1995). This is the memory for all the elements of an experience of which we are consciously aware at the time; all the sights, sounds, smells, conversations, even thoughts and images (Nadel & Moskowitz, 1997). This is what is typically thought of as memory, since when these memories are recalled they are expe-rienced as memory, i.e. as something remembered from the past. Explicit memory is further divided into semantic and episodic. Semantic memory is for general facts and knowledge (who is president) and personal facts and knowledge (where you were born). Episodic, also called autobiographical, memory is for spe-cific events (yesterday's visit to the dentist, last year's birthday celebration).

Brain structures involved in explicit memory

The modern era of understanding memory began in 1957 when a patient HM, aged 27, had both medial temporal lobes, MTL (which includes the hippocampal complex), surgically removed for treatment of intractable seizures (Neiser, 1967). Following the operation, while HM's intelligence remained normal, he had completely lost the ability to acquire new memories. He could hold new information for no more than a few moments. In other words, HM could not convert short-term/working memory into long-term memory. He would forget hospital staff he had just met, and even forget he had just eaten. This kind of memory loss is called anterograde amnesia, the inability to acquire new long-term memories in the period after the injury. Patients with MTL damage also have varying degrees of retrograde amnesia, the inability to recall memory from before the injury. For example, HM could not recall anything that had happened to him for the ten years before his lesion. However, he could remember his sixteenth birthday, which had occurred eleven years earlier. As a result of work with amnesic patients with MTL damage like HM, rats and monkeys, it is known that the MTL, particularly the hippocampal complex, is involved in the encoding, storage and retrieval of long-term explicit memory, that is, the memory of conscious experience (Mishkin, 1978; O'Keefe & Nadel, 1978; Zola-Morgan et al., 1989; Squire, 1992b). Although all the precise contributions to explicit memory of the MTL and other brain regions have not been completely worked out, some generally accepted ideas have emerged.

Memory is not actually stored in the hippocampus. It is stored in the same cortical sites that are involved in the original experiencing (Schacter, 1996). For example, the storage of the visual elements is in the occipital lobe and inferior temporal lobe. Storage of the sounds of words is in Wernicke's area of the temporal lobe. Eventually after some indefinite period of time, the connections in these cortical sites are strengthened, and the memory is said to be 'consolidated', which means that it is less susceptible to disruption and impairment (Squire & Zola-Morgan, 1991). After this cortical consolidation, the role of the hippocampus in retrieval wanes, as the strength of the cortical connections themselves are adequate to support retrieval. HM's ability to recall his sixteenth birthday, eleven years before the surgery, was presumably the result of these older memories having been consolidated, which meant that his hippocampus was no longer needed to retrieve them. While this has been the most widely accepted theory, more recent work (Joseph, 1996; Nadel & Moskowitz, 1997) suggests that the hippocampus continues to play some role in all explicit memory retrieval even after consolidation. To retrieve explicit memory, the hippocampal complex together with the frontal lobes serves as a kind of index that 'points to' the relevant information (sights, sounds, images etc.) that is stored in cortical sites, and holds them simultaneously in an activated state, which results in the experience of 'remembering' (Shimamura et al., 1991; Nadel & Moskowitz, 1997).

During the encoding of memory, the sensations and thoughts involved in conscious experience are provided by the primary and association cortices mentioned above. The spatial context of experience (where something happened) is specifically provided by the hippocampus and the temporal context (when it happened) by the prefrontal cortex. It is the spatial and temporal context added to the sensory elements of experience that convey the sense that these sensory elements have occurred as an 'episode' (Milner et al., 1985).

A balance exists between encoding events as completely unique episodes (meeting someone at a conference, but then the next day at a restaurant not realising it is the same person) and encoding the general aspects 'across' episodes (recognising a person in different situations). The hippocampus itself appears to be involved in encoding those elements of events that identify them as unique episodes, and other parts of the hippocampal complex encode elements that occur as more general aspects of experience (Vargha-Khadem et al., 1997).

All information comes from a source, either external (hearing about a good film from a friend at a party; learning about the French Revolution from a book) or internal (imagining you are lying on the beach in Hawaii; dreaming you forgot to take your final exam). The memory for the source of information is called source memory (Shimamura et al., 1991; Shimamura, 1995). Source memory often fades when remembering impersonal facts (remembering the name of the movie but forgetting where you found out about it). Crime reporting errors are often the result of flaws in source memory (Schacter, 1996). In one case a woman identified a particular man as having raped her. It turned out that she had in fact seen the man before, but not during the rape. She had seen him on television the night before the rape. As with working memory, source memory depends on the prefrontal cortex. Therefore, since children have immature prefrontal cortices they also are susceptible to source memory errors, which makes it difficult for them at times to discern whether information originates from within themselves (imagery, fantasy) or from external events.

Influences on encoding and retrieval of explicit memory

Encoding of memory is defined as the procedure for transforming what a person sees, hears, feels and thinks into memory. For explicit memory, encoding involves paying conscious attention to information. The particular way in which a person 'pays conscious attention' will impact on the subsequent recall of that information. For example, a process called 'elaborative' or 'deep' encoding involves consciously reflecting on information and making associations between what is to be remembered and information you already have (Kosslyn, 1994). To remember a list of words, you might pair each word with a visual image. 'Semantic' elaborative encoding is the making of conceptual associations with the information to be remembered. Subjects who are asked to remember a list of words, 'dog, floor, shirt, car' are more likely to remember the words if they make semantic, conceptual associations (dog is a type of animal) than if they make non-semantic associations (dog has only one vowel). During elaborative encoding, PET scan studies show increased blood flow to the prefrontal cortex (Kapur et al., 1994). This correlates with findings from neurology patients with lesions in the prefrontal cortex, who have difficulty with elaborative encoding.

Novelty of information enhances the likelihood that the information will be encoded explicitly (Tulving et al., 1994). It is assumed that novelty enhances explicit encoding, because increased conscious attention is generally given to novel aspects of the environment, as with a baby who cries for an object it can't have (like a precious vase) but is quickly distracted by a new object (a set of keys) towards which it now directs its conscious attention.

Emotionally arousing information and personally relevant information are more likely to be encoded than is neutral or irrelevant information (McGaugh, 1995; Cahill & McGaugh, 1995). Subjects who are shown films with emotionally arousing images and neutral images are more likely to remember the details of the emotionally arousing images. The impact of emotional arousal on encoding is mediated by 'stress hormone' (cortisol, epinephrine, norepinephrine) activation of the amygdala. Drugs that increase norepinephrine, for example amphetamines, enhance memory. Drugs that decrease norepinephrine, such as propranalol, impair memory. The amygdala itself does not do the encoding, but gives a signal to other areas involved in attentional focus and memory encoding, such as the hippocampus, when information is emotionally or otherwise significant to the organism, as if to say 'This information matters; pay attention to it and encode it!'

What enhances memory retrieval is the degree of similarity between the retrieval situation and the encoding situation (Tulving & Thompson, 1973). This is why memory is state-dependent. You are more likely to remember an event that was encoded during a sad mood if you are feeling sad. The closer particular aspects of the current situation, called retrieval cues, approximate to particular aspects of the encoding situation, the encoding cues, the more likely they are to elicit explicit recall of the memory. I lost a cheque that I was sure was somewhere in my house despite a thorough search. At the sight of my desk next morning, the whole memory flooded back of how I had sat at my desk in my office the week before trying to decide whether to take the cheque home or leave it in my desk. There it was in the desk. This occurs in analysis frequently, when for example, a particular word or gesture of the analyst calls to mind a vivid childhood memory in the patient that contains that or a closely related word or gesture. Even the high arousal state during a traumatic event can become encoded along with the event itself. In this way a subsequent high arousal state can serve as a retrieval cue to elicit the memory of the trauma.

The close relationship between encoding cues and retrieval cues explains why elaborative encoding is so effective for enhancing explicit memory. It provides more associative encoding cues, and therefore increases chances for retrieval cues to reinstate a memory. The more you think about how your current experience is linked with information you already know, the more likely you will be to recall that experience later. If you meet a person at a party, many of the cues used in the encoding of the experience of that party (what dress you wore, what food you ate) may call that person to mind if they occur on a subsequent occasion.

Explicit memory as a reconstructive process

Just as perception is a constructive process, memory retrieval is a reconstructive process (Joseph, 1996). The hippocampus-frontal 'index' joins together the individual sensory features, time and place of the experience to be remembered. What is remembered is constructed 'on the spot' and is not an exact replica of what happened in the past.

Since it is all the neural elements involved in the conscious processing of events that are encoded in explicit memory, consciously retrieved explicit memories themselves serve as new information to be stored as additional memory traces of the event (Nadel & Moskowitz, 1997). In fact, the more often an event is recalled the more memory traces there will be for that event, and the more opportunity for alteration of that memory, since each new retrieval event is a reconstructed phenomenon and not an exact duplicate of the original. The repeated re-telling of painful childhood events or conflicts during an analysis alter the memory of those events as more modified memory traces are laid down that include aspects of the therapeutic situation, and therefore they are somewhat less painful and conflicted, it is hoped.

NON-DECLARATIVE/IMPLICIT MEMORY

If declarative/explicit memory is the memory for the aspects of experience of which we are conscious, then by contrast non-declarative, also called implicit, memory is the memory for the aspects of experience that are non-consciously processed (Squire, 1992a). What this means is that certain information can be stored in memory without our having been consciously aware of its occurrence; it can non-consciously influence current functioning but does not feel like conscious remembering. Implicit memory includes the memory for shape and form (primed memory), emotion (emotional memory) and skills, habits and routines (procedural memory), each of which is processed in a different brain system. Implicit memory is almost always discussed 'as compared to' explicit memory, because scientists were aware of explicit remembering long before they were aware of the presence of implicit remembering. However, from an evolutionary perspective the brain systems that support procedural memory, the basal ganglia, were well developed in reptiles, whereas the hippocampal-based memory systems did not evolve except with lower mammals.

Priming

Priming means that prior exposure to words, sounds or shapes facilitates the subsequent identification or recognition of them from reduced cues or fragments (Schacter, 1992, 1995). Priming enhances recognition based on appearance or form and is independent of semantic meaning, which is an explicit memory function. The brain systems that subserve priming are the 'pre-semantic' perceptual centres in the posterior sensory cortex, such as the occipital lobe for visual priming, and are distinct from the centres involved in semantic meanings, which are more anterior. Brain-damaged patients with impaired semantic processing will still be able to read words yet they exhibit little or no understanding of them.

In a demonstration of priming, subjects study a list of low-frequency words, such as 'assassin' or 'parachute'. Subsequently they are tested for explicit memory by being asked if they recall the word being on the study list. Then they are tested for implicit memory with a word fragment completion test of words on the list, 'a—a—in' or '-ar-c-u-e', as well as words not on the list, such as '—e-s—x' (beeswax). Subjects show higher completion rates for word fragments of words on the study list than for words that were not on it. While this may not seem so surprising, what startled researchers is that subjects can more easily fill in the letters for words on the study list, even if on the explicit memory task they cannot consciously recall having seen the word on the list! Even subjects with amnesia from MTL lesions can show normal priming. Similar findings occur when the study list consists of novel 'made-up' shapes. Priming operates in each sensory domain separately. Therefore, while hearing a list of words will help subjects later to be able to recognise those words on a noisy tape recording, seeing those words previously will not help subsequent auditory recognition.

Priming not only enhances recognition of words and objects but alters judgments and preferences for them (Squire, 1992a). If told a list of proper names on a list are of famous people, subsequent exposure to those same names will reveal a greater likelihood that the names will be identified as 'famous'. Amnesic patients do as well as normal ones, although they have no conscious recall of seeing the names before. Subjects briefly exposed to a drawing, even for so brief a time that they are not conscious of having seen it, will be more likely to select that drawing later over other drawings that they were not exposed to previously. These priming effects can be long-lasting even after a single exposure. Schacter (1996) believes that auditory priming plays a role in infant preference and recognition of their mother's voice.

Procedural memory

Procedural memory is the memory for motor, perceptual and cognitive skills and habits (Squire, 1992a). Habits are behaviours that are built up gradually over many repetitions. Motor skills are things such as how to tie your shoes, ride a bike or play the piano. Cognitive skills are used for things such as learning an artificial grammar.

Procedural memory involves the basal ganglia; therefore the learning of skills and habits remains intact in amnesiac patients with MTL lesions. These patients can learn a motor skill through many hundreds of repetitions of the motor sequences involved, even though they cannot remember the sessions during which they learned the skill. One woman with MTL damage was taught through many repetitions a motor routine she could use for employment doing computer work, despite a complete lack of conscious recall for having learned how to do the job (Schacter, 1996). In animals, while the hippocampal-based 'context location' system of memory will help rats to find a specific location in a water maze, the basal ganglia procedural system will aid the recall of the specific motor actions required to reach the location. This means roughly that a rat with hippocampal damage will move through the maze with the same motor behaviours every time, no matter which 'start' position they begin from. Whereas rats with an intact hippocampus location learning swim directly to the location from whatever start position they are given (Nadel, 1992).

One test of habit learning is to present an image (such as a sun or clouds) followed by the presentation of four possible designs. Eventually a pattern emerges that is the probability that the sun, or cloud, will be followed by one of the four designs. By contrast, with patients with MTL lesions, who can learn these probabilities well but forget the learning sessions, patients with basal ganglia lesions, such as Parkinson's disease, show impaired 'probabilistic' habit learning but can perfectly recall the learning sessions (Knowlton et al., 1996). In addition, patients with basal ganglia damage, both with Parkinson's and with Huntington's disease, show impaired motor skill learning.

Some brain researchers (Grigsby & Hartlaub, 1994) theorise that what is considered a person's 'character', those things that people do routinely, automatically and unconsciously, may be mediated by procedural memory. What they suggest is that the repetition of any task, such as writing, throwing a ball, or even a way of interacting with others, can be supported by procedural memory systems once it becomes routinised and automatic, although at first it may involve conscious attention and the declarative, explicit memory systems. Calvin's (1996) work implies that it is adaptive for the brain to shift memory in this way. Since prefrontal cortical space is somewhat limited, it should be reserved for processing novel situations or ones that continue to need close attention. Routinised situations can be 'turned over' to other brain systems.

Emotional memory

Emotional memory is the conditioned learning of emotional responses to a situation and is mediated by the amygdala (LeDoux,

1994). Most work has been done on the conditioned fear response. Animals conditioned by a shock in conjunction with hearing a tone will later show a fear response, such as not moving at all, the 'freeze' response, when simply hearing the tone itself. Emotional conditioning occurs in humans as well (Bechara et al., 1995). Three patients were compared, one with a selective lesion of the amygdala, one with a hippocampal lesion and a patient with a combined amygdala and hippocampal lesion. These patients were shown red, green, blue or yellow slides. Occasionally the blue slide was accompanied by a startling loud noise. In normal subjects, this kind of loud noise typically produces an increase in the galvanic skin response (GSR). All three patients showed this response when hearing the loud noise. Normal controls are conditioned after seeing the blue slide paired with the loud noise several times, and show the increased GSR to the blue slide alone. The patient with hippocampal damage showed normal conditioning to the blue slide (an increase in GSR) but had no recall of the test event. The patient with damage to the amygdala remembered the test situation but failed to show any effect of conditioning (no increase in GSR). The patient with the combined lesion could neither recall the test situation nor show a conditioned GSR to the blue slide. LeDoux's (1995) work with rats shows that these fear responses can be rather enduring. Even after a long period in which the rat no longer experiences the tone paired with a shock, when one would expect that the fear response to the tone presented by itself would disappear or at least diminish, rats still can exhibit a forceful fear response to hearing the tone.

Emotion is a complex event, which will be more fully discussed in the next chapter. For the purpose of this discussion, however, the amygdala activation of emotion includes the visceral changes of the autonomic nervous system that accompany all emotion, such as changes in heart rate, gastric motility and vasodilation (LeDoux, 1995). The memory representations for these changes are stored separately from the factual details of the events.

Schacter (1996) theorises that implicit memory processed by the amygdala may be responsible for the way in which emotion can influence artists. One woman artist, following a severe fire in her flat, even when not consciously thinking about the fire, would continually paint images of flames and smoke for many years afterwards. By contrast, patients with amygdala damage may be impaired in the memory of feelings of fear.

CLINICAL IMPLICATIONS AND CONCLUDING REMARKS

Some important clinical implications for psychoanalysis regarding current neuroscience research on memory relate to the finding that explicit and implicit memory are processed differently and can become disconnected from one another. Clearly this has been observed with the neurologically damaged patients already mentioned. In what way may this be observed in patients with psychological conditions?

In the very early years of normal childhood, explicit memory is impaired because of the immaturity of the prefrontal cortex and hippocampus, whereas the basal ganglia and amygdala are well developed at birth (Joseph, 1996). This is part of the neuroscientific explanation for childhood amnesia. Theoretically there might be implicit memory for infant experiences, such as fears, somatic symptoms, or patterns of interaction derived from the mother–infant relationship, in the absence of explicit memory for this period.

The onset of verbal ability parallels the 'coming on line' of the hippocampus at 18 months. It is theorised that the narrative inter-actions between parents and children, when recounting the child's day at bedtime for example, enhance explicit memory processing for childhood events, by providing conscious attention to them (Nelson, 2000; Siegel, 1996). Perhaps people who have difficulty remembering their childhood may have lacked this aspect of the parent–child relationship. Nelson (2000) argues that although 2-year-old children evidence a rudimentary form of explicit memory, true explicit memory does not emerge until at least 3 years of age, when the relevant brain systems are more mature.

The majority of evidence regarding memory and psychological conditions involves patients with severe psychological trauma, from abuse, crime and war. Although, as McGaugh has demonstrated, emotional arousal enhances memory, it appears that excessively high levels of emotional arousal can actually impair memory. In rats, repeated stress can cause hippocampal atrophy (McEwen, 1995). In human beings as well, some patients with post-traumatic stress disorder (PTSD) have been noted to have decreased size of the hippocampus (Bremner et al., 1995). It is presumed that this is because of very high levels of circulating cortisol causing hippo-campal cell damage. As a result of hippocampal damage, trauma victims may have a number of memory impairments. They may incompletely recall the trauma, but retain the physical and emotional feelings associated with it. Or the events may be explicitly remembered while the implicit memories for them are expressed in a way that is disconnected from the events. One patient of mine, a victim of childhood sexual abuse, clearly recalled her trauma, but suffered intrusive 'somatic flashbacks', sensations of pounding vibrations and pressure on her chest that gave her difficulty breathing, which she did not experience as linked to the past trauma. One theory about flashbacks is that they are memories of the traumatic events without the location and temporal signature of hippocampal processing that would place them as events having occurred in the past. Instead of patients recognising them as past memories being reactivated in the present, they are experienced as happening in the 'here and now.' Another patient, who was raped on a brick pathway but amnesiac for the event, kept thinking of the words brick and path (Schacter, 1996). A visit to the rape scene made her emotionally distressed but she still could not remember the rape that occurred there. This patient may have become emotionally upset because of activation of her amygdala, although she had no explicit recall of the situation.

Therapeutically the verbalisation of traumatic symptoms, with the analyst's assistance in linking these up with past experiences of trauma, can facilitate explicit processing of trauma. This helps put the location and time signature on to these events. When these traumatic events are subsequently reactivated they can be felt more and more as the reactivation of past memory as opposed to current experience.

The dissociative defences used in trauma may also impair explicit memory for these events in a number of ways (Schacter,

1996). Dissociation resulting from altered states of consciousness can somehow sever the link between memory systems, so that memory is not erased but becomes detached from a person's conscious awareness. Dissociation can also involve directing conscious attention to neutral aspects of the scene, to avoid the overwhelmingly painful aspects of the trauma. The traumatic elements of the event may therefore not be well remembered in explicit memory, while the implicit somatic, emotional and behavioural aspects can remain intact. Fear can also cause hyperattention to frightening elements of the scene, such as occurs in crime situations when victims explicitly recall all the details about the gun, but have a poor memory for other details of the situation.

Repression may involve explicit memory that is blocked from being retrieved by the inhibitory affect of other information stored in long-term memory (Schacter, 1996). Also, the right frontal lobe may act to prevent particularly painful or unpleasant memories from gaining access to the left hemisphere in an attempt to protect verbal information processing (Joseph, 1996). During the period of repression of childhood conflicts there is reason to believe that implicit memory of childhood experience can still be expressed, through preferences, judgements, behaviours and emotions. Schacter himself translates the symptoms of the hysteric patients studied by Breuer and Freud into contemporary vocabulary. '[They] are plagued by implicit memories of events they cannot remember explicitly' (Schacter, 1996, p. 232).

However, since implicit memory is non-conceptual and non-linguistic it may be difficult to investigate it fully utilising the verbal free associative method. Some of the expansions of analytic enquiry such as analysis of countertransference reactions, the analyst's own reveries, empathic resonance and sensitivity to non-verbal communication are tools that may be better able to account for implicitly encoded experience.

No modern discussion of memory is complete without at least a mention of 'false memory', a topic of hot debate and controversy among neuroscientists. While space does not permit a complete review of the data on this issue, I will introduce a few of the arguments on both sides of the controversy. Essentially the question raised by the false memory issue is 'Can traumatic events that occur in childhood be completely forgotten and subsequently emerge as an accurate memory some time later in adulthood or are they simply false memories, implanted by a suggestion from a psychotherapist or else the product of the patient's own imagination?'

One side of the debate points to the findings that I have already presented. In a variety of ways trauma can impair the explicit encoding of information by hippocampal atrophy, dissociative defences that alter attentional mechanisms and disconnection between states of consciousness. In addition, repression, the impaired retrieval or recall of events, can occur through the inhibitory effects of other explicitly processed long-term memories and interference with right-to-left hemisphere transfer of information. Eventually, a current 'retrieval cue' may finally activate retrieval of the traumatic memory. As a result of these various mechanisms, explicit conscious recall of actual events may be impaired while implicit memory is retained. The implicit memory may result in 'symptoms' of trauma, such as emotions and somatic experiences, without the conscious recall of trauma.

The other side of the debate uses different data to argue that these 'repressed memories' can indeed be false. It is known that false information regarding events in a person's life can be implanted into both children and adults and then subsequently be 'remembered' as a true memory of the events (Schacter, 1996). For example, a child can be told that he was lost at the zoo. Even if no such event occurred, there is evidence that the child can subsequently not only 'remember' having been lost, but will embellish on this 'memory' with details of what they were wearing on the day they were lost and who the person was that found them! Even adult subjects in an experiment designed to test accuracy in reporting of details about the scene of an accident can be given falsely leading information that they subsequently remember as true. If it is suggested to them that there was a stop sign at the corner, even if no sign was present they can remember having 'seen' the sign. Further evidence on this side of the debate comes from PET scan studies (Schacter et al., 1996). Subjects first listen to a list of related words, such as 'bitter', 'taste', 'candy'. Later they look at a second list that contains some original words and different but related 'false target' words, such as the word 'sweet'. They are asked to identify which words on this second list they remember having heard before. No matter whether the word was one they heard on the original list or a 'false target' word, the PET scan shows activity in the hippocampus when subjects identify a word as one that they previously heard. When the word was one actually heard on the original list in addition to hippocampal activity, the PET scan shows activity in the auditory cortex. However, when they identify a 'false target' as a word they 'remember' hearing before, despite activity in the hippocampus, there is no activity in the auditory cortex, since they did not actually hear the word. It is postulated that it is activity in the hippocampus that gives 'memory' its sense of veracity, i.e. something that actually happened. By implication, when a patient reports a 'so-called' false memory of childhood abuse, they are expressing what they experience as true, despite the fact that the event may not have actually occurred.

Whether or not science is able to sort out the complex social, legal and moral dilemma of false memory syndrome remains to be seen. However, it already seems apparent that various aspects of the events we experience are not only processed in separate memory systems but can under certain conditions be activated or 'recalled' separately. For therapeutic purposes, clinicians need to be alert to possible implicit manifestations of prior experience that need to be consciously re-connected to the explicit details of these prior events.

REFERENCES

ALKON, D. (1992). *Memory's Voice*. New York: Harper Collins.

ATKINSON, R. C. & SHIFFRIN, R. M. (1968). Human memory: a proposed system and its control processes. In *The Psychology of Learning and Motivation: Advances in Research and Theory,* Vol. 2. New York: Academic Press, pp. 89-195.

BADDELEY, A. (1995). Working memory. In *The Cognitive Neurosciences*. Cambridge, MA: MIT Press, pp. 755-764.

—— & WARRINGTON, E. K. (1970). Amnesia and the distinction between long and short term memory. *J. Verb. Learn. Verb. Behav.,* 9: 176-189.

BEARDSLEY, R. (1997). The machinery of thought. *Scientific American*, August: 78-83.

BECHARA, A. ET AL. (1995). Double dissociation of conditioning and declarative knowledge relative to the amygdala and hippocampus in humans. *Science*, 269: 1115-1118.

BREMNER, J. D. ET AL. (1995). MRI based measurement of hippocampal volume in patients with combat related posttraumatic stress disorder. *Amer. J. Psychiat.*, 152: 973-981.

CAHILL, L. & MCGAUGH, J. L. (1995). A novel demonstration of enhanced memory associated with emotional arousal. *Consciousness & Cognition*, 4: 410-421.

CALVIN, W. H. (1996). *The Cerebral Code.* Cambridge, MA: The MIT Press.

FUSTER, J. M. (1994). *Memory in the Cerebral Cortex: An Empirical Approach to Neural Networks in the Human and Nonhuman Primate.* Cambridge, MA: MIT Press.

GRIGSBY, J. & HARTLAUB, G. H. (1994). Procedural learning and the development and stability of character. *Perceptual & Motor Skills*, 79: 355-370.

JOSEPH, R. (1996). *Neuropsychiatry, Neuropsychology and Clinical Neuroscience.* Baltimore, MD: Williams and Wilkins.

KAPUR, S. ET AL. (1994). Neuroanatomical correlates of encoding in episodic memory: levels of processing effect. *Proc. Nat. Acad. Sci. USA*, 91: 2008-2011.

KNOWLTON, B. J. ET AL. (1996). A neostriatal habit learning system in humans. *Science*, 273: 1399-1402.

KOSSLYN, S. M. (1994). *Image and Brain.* Cambridge, MA: MIT Press.

KUPFERMAN, I. (1991). Learning and memory. In *Principles of Neuroscience*. New York: Elsevier, pp. 997-1008.

LEDOUX, J. (1994). Emotion, memory and the brain. *Scientific American*, June: 50-57.

—— (1995). Emotion: clues from the brain. *Ann. Rev. Psychol.*, 46: 209-235.

MARKOWITSCH, H. J. (1995). Anatomical basis of memory disorders. In *The Cognitive Neurosciences*. Cambridge, MA: MIT Press.

MCEWEN, B. S. (1995). Stressful experience, brain, and emotions: developmental, genetic and hormonal influences. In *The Cognitive Neurosciences*. Cambridge: MIT Press, pp. 1117-1135.

MCGAUGH, J. L. (1995). Emotional activation, neuromodulatory systems and memory. In *Memory Distortion: How Minds, Brains and Societies Reconstruct the Past*. Cambridge: Harvard Univ. Press, pp. 255-273.

MILLER, E. K. ET AL. (1993). Activity of neurons in anterior inferior temporal cortex during a short term memory task. *J. Neurosci.*, 13: 1460-1478.

MILNER, B. ET AL. (1985). Frontal lobes and the temporal organization of memory. *Human Neurobiol.*, 4: 137-142.

MISHKIN, M. (1978). Memory in monkeys severely impaired by combined but not separate removal of amygdala and hippocampus. *Nature*, 273: 297-298.

NADEL, L. (1992). Multiple memory systems: what and why. *J. Cog. Neurosci.*, 4: 179-188.

—— & MOSKOWITZ, M. (1997). Memory consolidation retrograde amnesia and the hippocampal complex. *Current Opinion in Neurobiol.*, 7: 217-227.

NEISER, U. (1967). *Cognitive Psychology.* New York: Appleton, Century, Crofts.

NELSON, K. (2000). Memory and belief in development. In *Memory, Brain and Belief,* ed. D. L. Schachter and E. Scarry. Cambridge, MA: Harvard Univ. Press, pp. 259–89.

O'KEEFE, J. & NADEL, L. (1978). *The Hippocampus as a Cognitive Map.* Oxford: Clarendon Press.

SCHACTER, D. L. (1992). Priming and multiple memory systems: perceptual mechanisms of implicit memory. *J. Cog. Neurosci.,* 4: 244-256.

—— (1995). Implicit memory: a new frontier for cognitive neuroscience. In *The Cognitive Neurosciences.* Cambridge, MA: MIT Press, pp. 815-824.

—— (1996). *Searching For Memory.* New York: Basic Books.

—— & TULVING, E. (ED.) (1994). *Memory Systems 1994.* Cambridge, MA: MIT Press.

—— ET AL. (1996). Neuroanatomical correlates of veridical and illusory recognition memory: evidence from positron emission tomography. *Neuron,* 17: 1-20.

SHIMAMURA, A. P. (1995). Memory and frontal lobe function. In *The Cognitive Neurosciences.* Cambridge, MA: MIT Press, pp. 803-814.

—— ET AL. (1991). What is the role of frontal lobe lesions in memory disorders? In *Frontal Lobe Function and Dysfunction.* New York: Oxford Univ. Press, pp. 173-198.

SIEGEL, D. J. (1996). Cognition, memory and dissociation. *Child and Adolescent Psychiatric Clinics of North America,* 5: 509-536.

SQUIRE, L. R. (1992a). Declarative and nondeclarative memory, multiple brain systems supporting learning and memory. *J. Cog. Neurosci.*, 4: 232-243.

—— (1992b). Memory and the hippocampus: a synthesis from findings with rats, monkeys and humans. *Psychol. Rev*, 99: 143-145.

—— & ZOLA-MORGAN, S. (1991). The medial temporal lobe system. *Science*, 253: 1380-1386.

—— & KNOWLTON, B. J. (1995). Memory, hippocampus and brain system. In *The Cognitive Neurosciences*. Cambridge, MA: MIT Press, pp. 825–37.

TULVING, E. (1995). Organization of memory: quo vadis? In *The Cognitive Neurosciences*. Cambridge, MA: MIT Press, pp. 839-847.

—— ET AL. (1994). Novelty encoding networks in human brain positron emission tomography studies. *Neuroreport*, 5: 2525-2528.

—— & THOMPSON, D. M. (1973). Encoding specificity and retrieval processes in episodic memory. *Psychol. Rev*, 80: 352-373.

VARGHA-KHADEM, F. ET AL. (1997). Differential effects of early hippocampal pathology on episodic and semantic memory. *Science*, 277: 374-380.

ZOLA-MORGAN, S. ET AL. (1989). Lesions of perirhinal and parahippocampal cortex that spare the amygdala and hippocampal formation produce severe memory impairment. *J. Neurosci.*, 9: 4355-4370.

4: EMOTIONAL PROCESSING:
THE MIND–BODY CONNECTION

INTRODUCTION

From the evolutionary perspective first proposed by Darwin, emotions evolved to enhance survival by providing more adaptive solutions to problems that animals commonly encounter, such as maintaining body homeostasis, finding food, defending against danger, reproducing, caring for offspring and sustaining social relationships (Darwin, 1872; Pinker, 1997; LeDoux, 1996). Put in the simplest neuroscientific terms, emotions organise an animal's sustained responses to rewarding and aversive stimuli. The aim of this discussion is to illuminate the brain circuitry of emotion and show how these circuits apply to a wide variety of clinically relevant issues; anxiety, psychosomatic conditions, attachment and non-verbal communication.

The function of emotion is to co-ordinate the mind and body. Emotion organises perception, thought, memory, physiology, behaviour and social interaction so as to provide an optimal means for coping with the particular situation that is generating the emotion. Under the sway of fear, we are more likely to interpret stimuli as dangerous, have frightening thoughts, remember frightening things, show increased metabolic readiness to deal with danger, and to undertake behaviours such as 'freezing', fleeing or fighting to help avoid the threat. Infant emotions of separation distress organise the infant's bio-behavioural state so as to trigger comforting reunion responses in the care-taker. These examples illustrate a central thesis of this paper. Emotion connects not only the mind and body of one individual but minds and bodies *between* individuals.

Emotions begin simply. 'I feel sad.' Eventually they become better defined and are best described as the feelings one would have in particular situations; the sadness when a child dies or the sadness when a good friend moves away (Damasio, 1995).

The bridge between the neuroscience of emotion and psychoanalysis is that both centre on unconscious mechanisms. Neuroscience asserts that emotion is processed independently of conscious awareness; not in the dynamic unconscious of Freud but in a biological unconscious governed by the rules and constraints of neural circuitry and neurophysiology. Like psychoanalysis, neuroscience asserts that conscious feelings are but the tip of the iceberg. Truly meaningful information is often under the surface. For neuroscience, the physiological, behavioural and technological (PET scan, MRI etc.) findings are the manifest content of unconscious brain circuitry.

Claparède (1911) provided the first clinical demonstration that emotion can occur unconsciously. A female patient with brain damage, which today we assume included circuits involving the medial temporal lobe, was unable to form new memories. Each time Claparède visited her, he had to reintroduce himself. One day he experimented. While reintroducing himself along with his usual handshake, he held a pin in his hand. Although on subsequent occasions the woman still could not *consciously* remember him, she refused to shake his hand!

While people generally think of feelings as the reasons for behaviours ('I see a dog, feel afraid and therefore run away'), as far back as the 1880s, James (1884) proposed that feelings don't cause behavioural reactions, but that in part, behaviours cause feelings. We run, not because we are afraid, but we are afraid because we run. Although most of James's construct has now been discarded by current neuroscience, one aspect of his theory irrevocably changed human thinking about emotion, opening the way for modern theories. James proposed that the body changes that accompany the behaviour of running, such as racing heart, tight stomach and tense muscles, are perceived by the brain as bodily sensations, and contribute to what gives each emotion its unique quality.

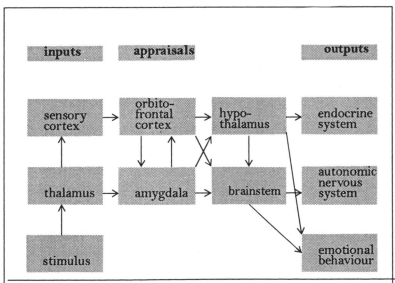

Figure 1: Emotion: a complex constellation of stimulus appraisals and biobehavioural responses.

A GENERAL SCHEMA OF EMOTIONAL PROCESSING

Although the actual picture is more complex, schematically emotion can be considered as a constellation of (a) stimulus appraisals as to their relevance to the organism, (b) brain and body changes that result from those appraisals and (c) feedback to the brain itself of those brain and body changes (LeDoux, 1996; Damasio, 1994, 1995; Joseph, 1996) (see Figure 1 above).

a) *Appraisal of stimuli*

Appraisal centres evaluate stimuli as to their overall significance for the organism. While only the amygdala and orbitofrontal cortex are discussed here, other appraisal centres do exist. For example, there is evidence that the amygdala preferentially appraises external stimuli and that the anterior insular cortex appraises internal stimuli such as thoughts and body sensations (Reiman, 1997).

At the most basic level stimuli can either be rewarding (e.g. food, sex) or aversive (e.g. thirst, predators). We tend to have positive emotions (e.g. happiness) about rewarding stimuli and negative emotions (e.g. fear) about aversive ones. It is considered that the amygdala makes more simple 'innately programmed' kinds of appraisals (is a stimulus good or bad? Familiar or unfamiliar? Safe or dangerous?) in response to simple stimulus cues such as large size, loud noise or wiggling motion. The orbitofrontal cortex reacts to the complex stimulus information of objects, people and events and makes appraisals that are built up from personal experience over the course of one's life.

The amygdala and orbitofrontal cortex are richly interconnected with cortical sensory and motor areas and subcortical limbic, mid-brain and brainstem regions. Therefore they are in the ideal position to sample, extract and add emotional attributes to ongoing experience.

(b) Brain and body changes

The amygdala and orbitofrontal cortex appraisal centres send messages to the hypothalamus and brainstem, which in turn activate the brain and body changes of emotion: endocrine production, autonomic nervous system responses and musculo-skeletal behaviours.

---

sympathetic nervous system (the 'fight or flight' system)
- eye — dilate pupil
- lung — increase respiration
- heart — increase heart rate
- salivary gland — inhibit salivation
- intestine — inhibit digestion
- adrenal medulla — release adrenalin

parasympathetic nervous system (the 'rest and digest' system)
- eye — constrict pupil
- lung — slow respiration
- heart — slow heart rate
- salivary gland — stimulate salivation
- intestine — stimulate digestion

Figure 2: The autonomic nervous system.

Endocrine production:

The hypothalamus regulates a number of hormones. The hypothalamus regulates cortisol levels, via the 'hypothalamic, pituitary, adrenal cortical axis', to facilitate the metabolic requirements of emotional arousal. The hypothalamus signals the pituitary to produce endorphins, which decrease pain sensations, and oxytocin or vasopressin, which promote attachment.

Autonomic responses:

The hypothalamus and brainstem regulate the autonomic nervous system, the part of the nervous system that innervates the internal viscera. The autonomic nervous system is divided into the sympathetic and parasympathetic nervous systems. Almost every organ is innervated by *both* the sympathetic and parasympathetic nervous systems, but with opposite effects (see Figure 2 above) (Schore, 1994). The sympathetic nervous system copes with external situations such as danger and is responsible for mobilising the fight or flight response. The parasympathetic nervous system focuses on the 'internal environment'; repair, reproduction, nutrition, growth and homeostasis. The sympathetic and parasympathetic nervous systems operate in tandem. An increase in heart rate can occur from increased sympathetic or decreased parasympathetic activity.

Musculoskeletal behaviours:

The hypothalamus and brainstem also control skeletal muscles via the cranial nerves and spinal cord to produce 'emotional' behaviours. Facial muscles contract in the facial expression of emotion (Ekman, 1990, 1993). Animals inhibit motor activity and 'freeze' during fear, to facilitate increased attention and orientation towards stimuli, and to decrease the chances of being detected by prey (Kapp et al., 1990).

There is good cortical control over skeletal muscle movement, less cortical control over the vocal cords and very little cortical control over autonomic innervation of the viscera (Ekman, 1991). Therefore, for example, we can mask our facial expressions of emotion (i.e. a poker face) but are less able to disguise a trembling voice and even less able to hide the 'flush' of embarrassment.

(c) Feedback of brain and body changes

It is theorised that these body and brain changes are fed back to the brain and are represented as part of the experience. Most of the time all of this proceeds without conscious awareness. When these changes are processed by those regions of the brain involved in producing consciousness (though what those regions are remains a hotly debated topic and will be discussed more fully in a subsequent article), they contribute to what we subjectively experience as our conscious emotions.

The terminology regarding emotion often differs from scientist to scientist. Damasio reserves the word 'feelings' for the responses of the body proper (e.g. contractions of the gut or flushing of the skin) that accompany the cognitive aspects of emotion (e.g. thoughts and imagery). Other researchers use the words 'feelings' or 'emotional feelings' to mean the (cognitive and somatic) totality of the conscious and subjective experience, which results from the underlying biological aspects of emotion.

Neuroscientists seem to use the words 'emotion' and 'affect' interchangeably, although the term 'affect' is sometimes reserved for the unconscious mental representation of the emotional process. Despite the fact that neuroscience does not specifically address affect as distinct from emotion, and although even within psychoanalysis the term affect is not consistently defined, it appears most likely that what is referred to by analysts as 'affect' is not just a mental state but a complex psychobiological state.

CONDITIONED FEAR AS A MODEL FOR EMOTIONAL PROCESSING

The brain circuitry of emotion is worked out in most detail in relation to fear, using fear conditioning to aversive stimuli as a research model (LeDoux, 1994, 1995, 1996). However, it is assumed that each emotion has its own particular circuitry. For example, specific nuclei in the amygdala and prefrontal cortex appraise rewarding stimuli and therefore are involved in the circuitry of positively toned emotions. While an emphasis on fear may seem a rather limited approach to emotion, the details of the fear system illustrate a central assumption of neuroscience. The body plays an active role in mental life!

Fear evolved to enhance detection and response to danger. All animals react with fear to extremely aversive stimuli such as shock. In addition each species has specific stimuli that elicit fear in that species. Rats react with fear to open spaces, vervet monkeys to eagles flying overhead. However, no matter what stimulus elicits fear, neural systems have been conserved throughout evolution. The brain structures, hormones, autonomic nervous system responses and behaviours of fear are similar in all animals. Therefore fear studied in rats or monkeys can reasonably be used to understand aspects of fear in human beings (Davis, 1992).

The classic fear conditioning experiment done in rats involves pairing a previously neutral stimulus, such as a tone, with a mild foot shock. The animal immediately exhibits the fear response, including 'freezing', increased startle reflex, defaecation, increased heart rate and cortisol. After only *one* exposure, the animal is conditioned to interpret the tone as aversive, meaning it will respond with the exact same fear response on subsequent occasions to the tone alone. Human beings also show this kind of rapid conditioning to mild shock. Once established, fear conditioning is relatively permanent, as illustrated by the results of extinction. When the tone is presented frequently *in the absence of shock*, eventually the fear

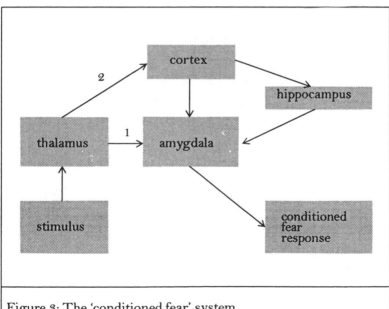

Figure 3: The 'conditioned fear' system.

response 'extinguishes'. However, the response is only inhibited, not erased completely. If the rat is exposed to some other unrelated stress, such as water deprivation, conditioned fear to the tone returns to its original intensity.

The details of fear circuitry emerge from experiments in which individual brain regions are lesioned and their effect on fear conditioning observed (LeDoux, 1994, 1995, 1996).

The role of the amygdala and cortex

The amygdala, *essential* for conditioned fear, is the hub of inputs and outputs. Two main *input* pathways are identified: (1) a rapid, shorter, subcortical route and (2) a slow, longer, cortical route (Figure 3 above) (see Chapter 2 for the relationship of these circuits to perception). Each elicits an identical *output*, the 'fear response', but in reaction to different stimulus information. In route (1) sensory information goes from the thalamus directly to the amygdala and rapidly triggers fear in response to simple stimulus cues. In route (2) sensory information is routed from the thalamus to the cortex and hippocampus and is then projected to the amygdala, taking longer to trigger fear in response to more complex stimulus objects.

What most surprised scientists is that the auditory cortex, which *is* required for conscious awareness of auditory stimuli is *not* required for conditioned fear! When the rat's auditory cortex is lesioned, fear conditioning still occurs, because subcortical route (1) remains intact, even though the animal cannot consciously hear the tone. The implication is that emotion can be triggered by situations of which the person is unaware.

Lesion studies reveal that although the cortex is not required to create a conditioned fear it plays a regulatory role in the process. The cortical route can inhibit a fear response triggered by the sub-cortical route. It also provides greater sensory discrimination. When two tones of different frequency are presented, but only one tone is paired to the shock, an animal with an intact auditory cortex reacts with fear *only* to the 'paired' tone. An animal with a lesioned auditory cortex reacts with fear to *both* tones. A cortical region called the medial prefrontal cortex is essential for extinction of fear. If this region is lesioned the rat's fear response to the tone will not be extinguished. These studies imply that although early fear responses to trauma may never completely disappear, conscious awareness may help diminish those fear responses.

Studies confirm the role of the amygdala in *human* fear. Stimulating the amygdala causes feelings of fear (Halgren, 1992). Removal of the amygdala for treatment of epilepsy causes impaired fear conditioning (La Bar et al., 1995). People normally react with fear to a loud obnoxious noise, just as rats and human beings do to shock. With an intact amygdala, when a soft noise is paired with a loud obnoxious noise, subjects subsequently react with autonomic arousal upon hearing the soft noise alone. Patients without an amygdala do not develop a conditioned response to the soft noise. Damage to the amygdala impairs recognition of fear on the faces of others while the ability to detect other emotions is retained (Bechara et al., 1995).

There are more connections from the amygdala to the cortex than from the cortex to the amygdala. This biases us towards fear, since automatic fear responses may be stronger than our ability to inhibit them volitionally.

The role of the hippocampus

The hippocampus provides information about contextual location (O'Keefe & Nadel, 1978; Phillips & LeDoux, 1992) (Figure 3 above). A rat in cage 'A' conditioned to a tone reacts with fear to the tone, but also reacts with fear when just placed in the cage! If later the rat is placed in cage 'B' and the fear response to the tone extinguished, the fear response will be elicited in full force by simply placing the animal back in cage 'A'. A man mugged once in front of his neighbour's house develops feelings of fear towards people who resemble the mugger, and also every time he walks past his neighbour's house. When the hippocampus is lesioned a rat still reacts with fear to the stimulus cue of the tone, but *not* to location cues of the cage. Contextual cues allow animals to learn to avoid danger even from cues only remotely related to danger, thus avoiding danger well before it happens. These findings imply that spatial cues activate fear in situations that are no longer dangerous, but in which the animal is merely in the same location as it was during a traumatic event. This may explain why rape victims assiduously avoid the specific situation (i.e. car park, flat) in which they were raped. Anything impairing the hippocampus can make fear generalise to other locations.

Besides its role in memory, the hippocampus also regulates emotional arousal, since cortisol binding of receptors in the hippocampus sends a message to the hypothalamus to slow the release of cortisol (Joseph, 1996; LeDoux, 1996). However, states of high excitation that cause excessive neocortical arousal can lead to diminished hippocampal activity, presumably to protect the neocortex from becoming overwhelmed. Emotionally traumatic events lead to very high levels of cortisol that can actually damage hippocampal cells (Bremner et al., 1995; Sapolsky, 1996). Therefore, dampening of hippocampal activity and actual hippocampal damage may lead to a loss of cortisol regulation and impairments in the memory of traumatic situations. Conversely, amygdala activity, if anything, *increases* during emotional arousal (Corodimas et al., 1994). These findings imply that at the same time stress may *impair* conscious explicit memory of a severe traumatic experience, it can *enhance* unconscious emotional memory of that experience!

How the prefrontal cortex chooses how to respond

The amygdala activates pre-packaged automatic responses. The prefrontal cortex, most developed in human beings, can shift from the automatic responses of the amygdala to decisions and choices about what response is indicated based on prior experience (Krasnegor et al., 1997). The prefrontal cortex, in relation to its working memory function (see Chapter 3 for a discussion of memory) anticipates the outcome of various response options and considers what might go wrong if one's plan fails. Human anxiety may be the high cost of the ability to anticipate danger and think about how things can go wrong, independent of them actually being present. Lower animals suffer the consequences of wrong choices but don't worry about it beforehand.

FEAR IN RELATION TO ANXIETY DISORDERS

The amygdala is most likely also the hub of human anxiety, since not only are the expressions of anxiety so similar to those of the fear

response—racing heart, increased respiration, dry mouth, diarrhoea, 'upset stomach', vigilance, jumpiness, easy 'startle', fidgeting
and apprehensive expectation—but the same brain regions that
produce the symptoms of anxiety also produce the signs of fear
(Davis, 1992). Pharmacological studies support Davis's proposal.
The amygdala is rich in both endorphin (opiate) receptors and benzodiazapines receptors. Direct infusion into the amygdala of either
opiate or benzodiazapine agonists both reduce expression of fear
conditioning and decrease anxiety in social interactions.

A confluence of factors related to fear conditioning is used by
neuroscientists to explain common clinical observations regarding
the emergence of anxiety, phobia and panic (Davis, 1992; LeDoux,
1996; Jacobs & Nadel, 1985).

No stimulus trigger may be evident in the current situation. A stimulus
in the current situation (i.e. smell, sound, object) may have been
conditioned during a prior danger situation to elicit a fear response
even in the absence of current danger, just as the tone did in the
experiments with rats. The current stimulus may be external such
as a sound or object, or internal such as a thought, image or fantasy.
Since conditioning can occur unconsciously through amygdala circuits, the person may not be aware of what the current stimulus
trigger is. Nevertheless, individuals typically explain their anxiety
in terms of something in the current environment that makes sense,
such as anxiety about getting stuck in a lift.

Stress from whatever cause (i. e. illness, loss of a loved one) appears to make
people susceptible to developing anxiety attacks, phobias and panic conditions,
and may cause these conditions to spread or intensify. During stress the
hippocampus may become impaired or even damaged, while amy-

gdala activity can be enhanced (LeDoux, 1996; Bremner et al., 1995; Sapolsky, 1996). This increases conditioned fear, but without the hippocampus to provide contextual specificity to fear learning or adequate explicit memory for traumatic events. Therefore these conditioned fears may spread to other kinds of situation (dogs, driving the car, going out of the house) even while the individual remains unaware of the original traumatic situation that may have elicited them.

Anxieties and phobias so often involve insects, snakes, contamination and heights. Presumably the amygdala contains 'prepared' fears, meaning innate fears 'handed down' through evolution, which do not require a prior experience of danger. A baby monkey runs from a wiggling rope even if it has never seen a snake. During stress, if the hippocampus is impaired and the amygdala enhanced, these 'prepared fears' may emerge spontaneously as insect or snake phobias, without assuming a traumatic exposure to the feared object.

Once anxiety attacks or phobias emerge they can escalate into panic states. The symptoms of anxiety themselves (i.e. racing heart, sweaty palms), by association with the danger situation, can themselves be conditioned to elicit a fear response. This may begin a vicious cycle in which a mild anxiety attack can elicit another and another, and even spiral into panic. Another contribution to this vicious cycle is that internal sensors of body homeostasis exist, measuring for example blood volume and CO_2 levels (Svensson, 1987). These sensors can trigger a fear response in reaction to 'internal cues' of physiological imbalance. Therefore any situation, even the normal arousal of a novel situation or physical exertion can trigger an anxiety attack, which in the predisposed individual may lead to runaway stress or even panic states.

The human hippocampus is immature in the first two years of life, while the amygdala is fully developed. Jacobs & Nadel (1985) suggest that by virtue of this fact, during severe stress resulting in hippocampal damage in adult life, *very early* infantile fears can re-emerge that have been retained in the emotional memory of amygdala circuits.

The price of adaptation

In some ways emotional processing seems less than adaptive. Fears once established are almost impossible to eliminate and early, over-generalised, learning can interfere with current functioning. These factors cause human beings to suffer neurotic fears. However, these same factors serve important adaptive functions. When it comes to danger, it is helpful for the animal only to have to learn it once. Also, early learning needs to be highly generalised. For example, the infant needs to generalise learning of the mother's smell and appearance to all situations with mother not just particular ones. Context-specific information about location may not be required until locomotor abilities emerge (coincidentally at the same time the hippocampus matures), and the infant can explore a variety of places.

EMOTION AND PSYCHOSOMATIC CONDITIONS

It is apparent from the connection between emotion and hormonal, visceral and musculo-skeletal body responses, how emotion leads to actual *physical* changes that can contribute to psychosomatic and other 'somatising' disorders. No longer can physicians tell patients, 'It is all in your head', since anything 'all in the *head*' *is* also in a sense 'all in the *body*'. Chronic high levels of autonomic arousal can lead to chronic *physical* symptoms of anxiety, such as muscle tension, palpitations, increased blood pressure, difficulty breathing, diarrhoea, and may ultimately damage body tissues such as the cardiovascular system. The autonomic nervous system regulation of lung and intestinal function may play a role in such conditions as asthma and irritable bowel syndrome. Chronic high levels of cortisol can impair the immune system, and contribute to ulcer formation.

Cognitive complaints such as impaired memory, diminished concentration, difficulty with thinking and responding coherently or simply feeling 'fuzzy' in the head often accompany intense emotion and stress-related illness. These cognitive impairments may result from a variety of brain alterations that occur during emotional arousal. Hippocampal cells can show diminished activity or even atrophy during stress, leading to disruptions of attention and memory (Sapolsky, 1996; LeDoux, 1996). In response to external danger, stimulus processing shifts away from the frontal cortex, responsible for focused attention, motivation and monitoring of goals, to the posterior cortex, responsible for vigilance to external stimuli (Krasnegor et al., 1997). The reduced frontal activity found on PET scans in severely depressed patients may contribute to the apathy and lack of concentration associated with major depression (Biver et al., 1994). Lastly, when receptors detect homeostatic imbalances in the viscera, attention to internal stimuli overrides attention to the external world (Svensson, 1987).

How Regulation of Emotion is *Essential* for Health

Emotional arousal is not harmful *per se,* since embedded in the normal emotional processes are the means for regulating arousal. It is only *dys*regulated emotion that is harmful. In fact *not enough* emotion is just as maladaptive as too much. For example in one study, Henry (1993) identified a group of individuals who, under stress, show overt signs of distress, have an increase in cortisol and turn to others for support as they experience an inability to cope with the situation. These *adaptive* individuals show autonomic stability. He identified another group who do not appear overtly distressed, do not exhibit *enough* cortisol response to stress and do not turn to others for support. These *impaired* individuals exhibit autonomic over-arousal. Henry postulates that because these impaired individuals do not overtly experience distress and lack the rise in cortisol, they do not turn to others to help them regulate their over-aroused autonomic nervous system.

A variety of studies reveals that some infants are born with more of an ability to self-soothe and be soothed by others when emotionally distressed. Other infants are born with less self-soothing ability and are less able to be soothed by others, thereby predisposing these infants to *dys*regulated emotion. Healthy newborns need to react to stress by mobilising maximal attention and information processing and yet be able to maintain homeostasis as well. Healthy babies react to stress with a rise in cortisol but then can automatically use quiescence to 'recover from stress' and reduce cortisol (Gunnar, 1992). Porges (1992) has identified that healthy term infants have high vagal tone (slowing the heart rate via parasympathetic nervous system activity) but that they suppress vagal tone, at the same time as they increase sympathetic nervous system, in situations requiring emotional reactivity. Healthy babies who are distressed can be distracted and at least temporarily soothed, since the shift of attention to a novel stimulus activates the orienting response, which includes behavioural calming, allowing infants to be optimally responsive to new information from the environment (Krasnegor et al., 1997). These findings in babies reflect a general principle; healthy individuals react with emotional arousal to environmental situations in a co–ordinated fashion that maximises attention and information processing, but return to a calm state afterwards in order to maintain homeostasis.

Two groups of babies have been identified that are impaired from birth in these normal self-regulatory mechanisms. A group of infants labelled 'regulatory disordered' do not suppress vagal tone in situations requiring emotional arousal. These infants are fussy, irritable, show poor self-calming, intolerance to change and hyper-alert arousal, and share many characteristics of infants described as having a fussy temperament (Degangi et al., 1991). Another group of infants characterised as 'shy' or 'inhibited' temperament are difficult to soothe and show dysregulation of emotion in novel situations. A normal infant who is distressed will be calmed by the distracting measures used by parents. The infant with 'inhibited temperament', however, is not calmed by distraction. What leads to decreased 'soothability' in the 'inhibited temperament' is the *in-ability* to shift attention efficiently when orienting to novel stimuli. Infants with emotional dysregulation can show lifelong consequences, such as attentional problems and learning difficulties.

EMOTIONAL PROCESSING IN RELATION TO ATTACHMENT

The phenomenon of attachment and the discussion on non-verbal communication that follows illustrate how the same mechanisms that activate brain and body responses to stimuli during emotional processing *within* an individual can link brain and body responses *between* individuals as well. Attachment and non-verbal communication are examples of how individuals regulate both one another's biology and psychology. Attachment has been well studied as a psychological phenomenon. Neuroscience contributes the finding that attachment is also a biological phenomenon.

Mother-infant attachment

Attachment is crucial, since mammals depend on maternal care for survival. Attachment involves proximity-seeking, distress on separation and comfort on reunion, and results from maternal attunement to a spectrum of infant biological states as well as affect states (Hofer, 1995; Schore, 1994). Attachment involves a delicate feedback loop in which mother and infant regulate each other. Each mammalian species exhibits separation and reunion behaviours that characterise attachment for that species. The 'distress cry' upon separation is universal to mammals (Hofer, 1995; Kalin et al., 1995). The biological mechanisms of attachment identified in animals are believed to apply to human attachment as well.

Hofer (1995), studying rats, identifies specific maternal factors that regulate infant factors. The mother's milk supply maintains the young rat's heart rate. Tactile contact with mother (i.e. licking) maintains the rat's body temperature and activity level. Upon separation the young rat's heart rate, temperature and activity level decrease.

A series of interacting infant and maternal responses occur when a rat is separated from its mother. In the infant, separation *automatically* elicits the 'separation response'—a distress cry (using the same laryngeal muscles as in human crying), huddling together with litter mates and following the mother. On hearing the distress call, the mother *automatically* initiates the 'search and retrieve' response. She looks for the baby rat, picks it up, returns it to the nest and immediately begins licking and providing milk. Reunion closes the feedback loop and the 'separation response' diminishes.

The separation response of the human infant also involves distress behaviours and physiological dysregulation (Hofer, 1996). When babies are separated from their mother they exhibit a characteristic 'protest phase', which includes separation distress behaviours such as crying, followed by a 'despair phase' if the mother does not return, which results from physiological dysregulation, such as a slowed heart rate and decreased activity level. Hofer believes that attachments function as biological regulators even between adult–adult dyads. When a spouse dies, the acute grief stage with overt crying, sighing, postural and facial expressions of sadness may be followed by dysregulation of biological systems, such as cardiovascular disease, endocrine and immune system impairments, leaving the remaining spouse more susceptible to illness and death.

The separation response is mediated by benzodiazapine receptors in the amygdala (Davis, 1992). Infusions into the amygdala of benzodiazapine receptor agonists decrease infant distress crying even

upon separation, while infusions of benzodiazapine receptor antago-
nists increase infant distress even in the absence of separation.

'Reunion responses' have been extensively studied in monkeys
(Kalin et al., 1995). Monkey reunion behaviours involve clinging to
one another and a type of vocalisation called 'girning'. Based on a
series of experiments, Kahn proposes that reunion is mediated
through the amydala 'opiate'/endorphin receptor system. Monkey
babies and mothers each are injected with either naltrexone (an opiate antagonist) or morphine (an opiate agonist). Naltrexone in both
infants and mothers increases reunion behaviours, presumably to
increase endogenous opiate levels. Morphine, on the other hand,
decreases re-union behaviours in infants and mothers, presumably
in order to 'down regulate' high endorphin levels. Kalin theorises
that endorphins are released during reunion behaviours and serve
to reinforce attachment/reunion, in a sense addicting us to attachment figures.

Until recently, oxytocin and vasopressin released by the hypothalamus were considered only in relation to reproduction (oxytocin)
and water metabolism (vasopressin). Insel (1997) proposes that
these two hormones also play a role in male/female pair bonding in
monogamous species. Insel's work with a species of monogamous
voles called the prairie vole shows that they exhibit a characteristic
hormonal pattern not evident in *non-monogamous* voles. The female
prairie vole releases oxytocin during mating, which causes her to
bond specifically to her mating partner. The male prairie vole
releases vasopressin upon mating. This prompts a mating preference for this single female and leads to aggressively defending her
from intrusion by other males.

EMOTION AND NON-VERBAL COMMUNICATION

While most of psychoanalytic literature has focused on the unconscious symbolic meanings of non-verbal communication (Jacobs, 1994), neuroscience emphasises the unconscious influence that one person's non-verbal communication has on another's biology, emotion and verbal conversation. Neuroscientific findings reveal that non-verbal communication of emotion, as is well illustrated by attachment, regulates minds and bodies between individuals. Just as neurotransmitters transfer information from the pre-synaptic membrane to the post-synaptic membrane, non-verbal communications, like the distress cry, carry information about bio-emotional states between individuals, thus regulating the biological functioning of both people.

Non-verbal communication includes facial expression, gesture, posture and vocal prosodic elements such as tone, rhythm and quality of speech (Ekman, 1990, 1993). Ekman proposes innate emotions universal to all human beings. While there is controversy on just which emotions these are, there is general agreement that some innateness of emotional expression does exist. Even babies blind and deaf from birth show the full array of normal facial expressions.

Ekman believes there is a close link between facial expression (striatal muscle), autonomic modulation of body functions (visceral muscle) and subjective feelings associated with emotion. In happiness and surprise (the positive emotions) and anger, fear, sadness and disgust (the negative emotions), Ekman (1990, 1993) identifies specific muscle group contractions that create each of the facial expressions associated with these emotions. Measuring an array of autonomic responses such as heart rate, galvanic skin response and skin temperature, Ekman demonstrates that when subjects are instructed to imagine a situation in which they would feel a particular emotion they exhibit a pattern of autonomic changes that characterise that emotion. Even more fascinating, when subjects are instructed *only to contract* the specific muscle groups associated with a specific emotion there is a high percentage of subjects who actually *feel* that emotion and *demonstrate the autonomic changes* associated with it. Ekman believes the autonomic changes are responsible for the subjective feelings of emotion and serve as the biological support for the behaviours associated with the emotion. For example, anger and fear show an increase in heart rate, while happiness and surprise do not. The increased heart rate supports the defensive behaviours of fighting or running that occur with danger and threat.

Ekman's work sheds light on the biology of empathic attunement (Beebe & Lachmann, 1988). Infants and mothers spontaneously attune to one another's emotional states by matching the facial expression, tone of voice and behaviours. A number of experiments show that adults also spontaneously match non-verbal cues with one another, generating emotional attunement between adults. In experiments, adult subjects who match non-verbal cues while talking together are more likely than subjects who do not match cues to feel a sense of rapport with one another (Feldstein & Welkowitz, 1978). On a psychiatric ward, when staff spontaneously match the rhythm and prosody of speech of psychotic patients, these patients are less likely to be labelled 'difficult' (Freedman & Lavender, 1997). Beebe & Lachmann propose that when one individual matches another's non-verbal and facial expression, this recreates inside that person the autonomic changes and body sensations associated with the other's emotional state. We may literally feel what another feels.

Non-verbal communication is fundamental to all forms of social interaction (Brothers, 1989). Social animals such as monkeys and human beings rely on being able to know what another feels and what their intentions are. Are they feeling angry? Sad? Interested? Are they intending to eat? Mate? Or play? The non-verbal expression of emotion and intention are processed by regions such as the amygdala and orbitofrontal cortex. Individual cell recordings while monkeys are watching others of the same species in a variety of natural movements reveal that individual cells in these regions are selectively responsive to individual cues. Some cells are sensitive to direct eye contact, others to faces in profile. Some are sensitive to eyebrow position or whether a mouth is yawning, baring teeth or eating. These cues form the complex communications of emotion and intent.

Non-verbal cues are used to manage social relationships, and activate responses in others (Tomkins, 1963). Direct eye contact increases aggression between unfamiliar individuals. A child in an abject state of shame lowers its head, which activates attempts by the mother to repair the shame state (Schore, 1994). Crying in adults appears to activate sympathy and comforting responses in others (Gross et al., 1994). Alexithymic patients suffer autonomic over-arousal as a result of impairments in utilising others as 'self-regulators' (Troise et al., 1996). This is because they are not only impaired in the verbal expression of emotion, but in the non-verbal expression as well. Because of their lack of non-verbal expressions of distress, they do not engender soothing responsiveness in others.

Non-verbal communication also unconsciously structures all forms of verbal exchange (Kendon, 1992). In conversation, unconscious non-verbal cues normally signal whose turn it is to talk, who is talking to whom and when the subject is changing.

CONCLUSION: 'I FEEL THEREFORE I AM'

Rational decision-making is not so rational after all (Damasio, 1994). Emotion plays an important role in judgement and reason. The orbitofrontal cortex, a region of the prefrontal cortex, is able to utilise prior emotionally significant experiences in such a way that it can flexibly apply that information to current functioning. In a current situation the orbitofrontal cortex has access to the representations of body responses from prior situations and these body responses influence how the individual will respond to the current situation. Damasio's theory derives from patients with orbitofrontal cortex damage. These patients demonstrate both poor judgement and abnormalities of autonomic responses to emotion, such as lack of increased GSR during emotional arousal. Sociopaths, who also show poor judgement, show impairment of GSR to emotional arousal as well.

Bechara et al. (1997) use a card game with two 'stacked' decks to study how these patients are impaired in decision-making. Subjects turn over a card indicating either a 'win' or 'loss' of money. In the 'good' deck, the gains are small but so are the losses and the individual prospers in the long run. In the 'bad' deck, the rewards are big but the losses even bigger and the person eventually loses everything. Subjects are free to turn over cards in either deck. Eventually, after turning over several cards, subjects with a normally functioning orbitofrontal cortex begin to select just from the 'good' deck, making this choice *before* they are consciously aware of the differences between the two decks. Subjects with damage to the orbitofrontal cortex keep picking cards from the 'bad' deck. Even though they are eventually able to be consciously aware of the difference, they do not seem to care. They simply do not utilise this information to affect their choices. Damasio proposes that emotional memory, represented as body changes, influences choice-making outside conscious awareness. Might this be the intuitive 'gut' response?

What neuroscience emphasises is that emotion and the expression of emotion are involved in all important human endeavours, even those not previously considered emotional such as rational decision-making. What these neuroscientific findings suggest is that emotional non-verbal exchange may play at least as much importance in analytic treatments as does verbal exchange. Analysts and patients may influence one another's body sensations, imagery, thoughts, behaviours and even words by unconsciously processed non-verbal cues of emotion, such as autonomic changes (i.e. flushing, dry mouth) and behaviours (i.e. facial expression, posture, gesture). These cues are vital data from the analyst as well as from the patient. How the analyst *feels*, both 'in the body' and 'in the mind', may be as important an indicator of what is going on in the patient as whatever the analyst is thinking. *How* the analyst communicates may be as important as *what* the analyst says (Pally, 1996). In fact even how the analyst *behaves* may be as much of an indicator of what is going on unconsciously in the patient as anything that is consciously known by either individual.

To conclude, neuroscience supports the clinical wisdom that patients are helped if they can feel their feelings and express them to others. Emotion facilitates adaptive behaviours, contributes to adaptive problem-solving and organises important social relationships. However, emotional arousal needs to be regulated. The conscious awareness of emotion and emotional expression to others both play a role in the regulation of emotional arousal that is so important to healthy functioning.

REFERENCES

BECHARA, A. ET AL. (1995). Double dissociation of conditioning and declarative knowledge relative to the amygdala and hippocampus in humans. *Science*, 269: 1115-1118.

—— (1997). Deciding advantageously before knowing the advantageous strategy. *Science*, 275: 1293-1294.

BEEBE, B. & LACHMANN, F. M. (1988). The contributions of mother–infant mutual influence to the origins of self and object representations. *Psychoanal. Psychol.*, 5: 305-337.

BIVER, F. ET AL. (1994). Frontal and parietal metabolic disturbances in unipolar depression. *Biol. Psychiat.*, 36: 381-388.

BREMNER, J. D. ET AL. (1995). MRI-based measurement of hippocampal volume in patients with combat-related posttraumatic stress disorder. *Amen J. Psychiat.*, 152: 973-981.

BROTHERS, L. (1989). A biological perspective on empathy. *Amer. J. Psychiat.*, 146: 10-19.

CLAPARÈDE, E. (1911). Recognition and 'me-ness'. In *Organisation and Pathology* of *Thought*. New York: Columbia Univ. Press, pp. 58-75.

CORODIMAS, K. P. ET AL. (1994). Corticosterone potentiation of learned fear. *Annals* of *the New York of Sciences*, 746: 392-393.

DAMASIO, A. R. (1994). *Descartes' Error*. New York: Putnam.

—— (1995). Toward a neurobiology of emotion and feeling: operational concepts and hypotheses. *The Neuroscientists*, 1: 19-25.

DARWIN, C. (1872). *The Expression of the Emotions in Man and Animals*. Chicago, IL: Univ. Chicago Press, 1965.

DAVIS, M. (1992). The role of the amygdala in fear and anxiety. *Ann. Rev. Neurosci.*, 15: 353-375.

DEGANGI, G. A. ET AL. (1991). Psychophysiological characteristics of the regulatory disordered infant. *Behavior Devel.*, 14: 37-50.

EKMAN, P. (1990). Voluntary facial action generates emotion specific autonomic nervous system activity. *Psychvphysiol.*, 27: 363-383.

—— (1991). Who can catch a liar? *Amer. Psychologist*, 46: 913-920.

—— (1993). Facial expression and emotion. *Amer. Psychologist*, 48: 384-392.

FELDSTEIN, S. & WELKOWITZ, J. (EDS) (1978). *A Chronography* of *Conversation. Nonverbal Behavior and Communication*. Hillsdale, NJ: Lawrence Erlbaum.

FREEDMAN, N. & LAVENDER, J. (1997). Receiving the patient's transference: the symbolizing and desymbolizing countertransference. *J. Amer. Psychoanal. Assn.*, 45: 79-104.

GROSS, J. J. ET AL. (1994). The psychophysiology of crying. *Psychophysiol.*, 31: 460-468.

GUNNAR, M. (1992). Reactivity of the hypothalamic-pituitary-adrenocortical system to stressors in normal infants and children. *Pediatrics*, suppl.: 491-497.

HALGREN, E. (1992). Emotional neurophysiology of the amygdala within the context of human cognition. In *The Amygdala: Neurobiological Aspects of Emotion, Memory and Mental Dysfunction.* New York: Wiley-Liss, pp. 191-228.

HENRY, J. P. (1993). Psychological and physiological responses to stress: the right hemisphere and the hypothalamo-pituitary-adrenal axis, an inquiry into problems of human bonding. *Physiol. & Behav. Sci.*, 28: 369-387.

HOFER, M. A. (1995). Hidden regulators. In *Attachment Theory: Social, Developmental and Clinical Perspectives.* Hillsdale, NJ: Analytic Press, pp. 203-230.

——— (1996). On the nature and consequences of early loss. *Psychosomatic Medicine*, 58: 570-581.

INSEL, T. (1997). A neurobiological basis of social attachment. *Amer. J. Psychiat.*, 154: 726-735.

JACOBS, T. (1994). Nonverbal communications: some reflections on their role in the psychoanalytic process and psychoanalytic education. *J. Amer. Psychoanal. Assn*, 42: 741-762.

JACOBS, W. J. & NADEL, L. (1985). Stress-induced recovery of fears and phobias. *Psychol. Rev.*, 92: 512-531.

JAMES, W. (1884). What is an emotion. *Mind*, 9: 188-205.

JOSEPH, R. (1996). *Neuropsychiatry, Neuropsychology and Clinical Neuroscience.* Baltimore, MD: Williams and Wilkins.

KALIN, N. H. ET AL. (1995). Opiate systems in mother and infant primates coordinate intimate contact during reunion. *Psychoneuroendocrinol.*, 20: 735-42.

KAPP, B. S. ET AL. (1990). A neuroanatomical systems analysis of conditioned bradycardia in the rabbit. In *Learning and Computational Neuroscience: Foundations of Adaptive Networks.* Cambridge, MA: MIT Press, pp. 53-90.

KENDON, A. (ED.) (1992). The negotiation of context in face-to-face interaction. In *Rethinking Context: Language as an Interactive Phenomenon.* London: Cambridge Univ. Press, pp. 323-334

KRASNEGOR, N. ET AL. (EDS) (1997). *Development of the Prefrontal Cortex.* Baltimore, MD: Paul Brookes.

LA BAR, K. S. ET AL. (1995). Impaired fear conditioning following unilateral temporal lobectomy in humans. *J. Neurosci.*, 15: 6846-6855.

LEDOUX, J. (1994). Emotion, memory and the brain. *Scientific American*, 270: 32-39.

―― (1995). Emotion: clues from the brain. *Ann Rev. Psychol.*, 46: 209-235.

―― (1996). *The Emotional Brain.* New York: Simon and Schuster.

O'KEEFE, J. & NADEL, L. (1978). *The Hippocampus as a Cognitive Map.* Oxford: Clarendon Press.

PALLY, R. (1996). Reciprocal responsiveness and the matching of nonverbal clues in psychoanalysis. *J. Clin. Psychoanal.*, 5: 7-23.

PHILLIPS, R. G. & LEDOUX, J. E. (1992). Differential contribution of amygdala and hippocampus to cued and contextual fear conditioning. *Behavioral Neurosci.*, 106: 274-285.

PINKER, S. (1997). *How the Mind Works.* New York: W. W. Norton.

PORGES, S. W. (1992). Vagal tone: a physiologic marker of stress vulnerability. *Pediatrics*, 90: 498-504.

REIMAN, E. M. (1997). The application of positron emission tomography and the study of normal and pathological emotion. *J. Clin. Psychiat.*, 58 (suppl. 16): 4-12.

SAPOLSKY, R. M. (1996). Why stress is bad for your brain. *Science*, 273: 749-750.

SCHORE, A. N. (1994). *Affect Regulation and the Origin of the Self.* Hillsdale, NJ: Lawrence Erlbaum.

SVENSSON, T. H. (1987). Peripheral, autonomic regulation of locus ceruleus noradrenergic neurons in brain: putative implications for psychiatry and psychopharmacology. *Psychopharmacol.*, 92: 1-7.

TOMKINS, S. (1963). *Affect/Imagery/Consciousness Tool. 2. The Negative Affects.* New York: Springer.

TROISE, A. ET AL. (1996). Nonverbal behavior and alexithymic traits. *J. Nerv. Ment. Dis.*, 184: 561-566.

5: BILATERALITY: HEMISPHERIC SPECIALISATION AND INTEGRATION

INTRODUCTION

The two cerebral hemispheres are identical in appearance. However, ever since Broca discovered in 1861 that left hemisphere damage results in 'expressive' aphasia, neuroscientists have realised that the brain is functionally asymmetrical (Ornstein, 1997). A few years later, Wernicke identified that left hemisphere damage leads to 'receptive' aphasia. As a result, neuroscientists held the belief that the left hemisphere was superior to the right because it was the language centre, and thus the seat of reason and intellect. Eventually, however, Hughlings-Jackson, in the 1870s, realised that the right hemisphere plays a central role in comprehension of the world *together with* the left. During this same period, many neuroscientists were influenced by popular notions regarding the essential nature of man, such as those depicted in Robert Louis Stevenson's 1886 story of *Dr Jekyll and Mr Hyde*. For these neuroscientists, it was as if humans had two separate minds, even two 'consciousnesses', a 'cultivated' left one and a 'primitive' right one.

In this century, in the 1930s, Lange revitalised interest in the central importance of the right hemisphere. He recognised that the right hemisphere provides a general contextual background to a person's world view. During the 1960s the initial work of Sperry and Gazzaniga (Gazzaniga et al., 1962) at first seemed to corroborate the 'two minds, two consciousnesses' view held by some late nineteenth-century scientists. Subsequent work, however, resulted in the now generally accepted 'asymmetric but integrated' perspective. The right and left cerebral cortex are each lateralised for specialised functions, but in the healthy brain the two hemispheres share their information and operate collaboratively (Joseph, 1996; Deacon, 1997; Gazzaniga, 1995; Ornstein, 1997).

Research regarding lateralisation of specialised functions pertains mostly to *cortical* functions. However, it must be remembered that specialised functions of each cortex are influenced by input from *subcortical* structures as well as from other cortical sites in the same or opposite hemisphere. According to Deacon, functional asymmetry evolved because in certain circumstances organisms must prioritise, and have only one goal, express only one action, or speak only one thought. For these particular functions only *one* hemisphere must have the advantage.

Neuroscientists assume that the reason that language and fine motor movements are lateralised to the left cerebral cortex and emotion and musical ability to the right cerebral cortex is a fundamental difference between the left and right cortices with respect to information processing (Galin, 1974; Tucker, 1981). The left is better at analysing rapid temporal-sequential aspects of information. Therefore the left hemisphere more readily identifies 'details' and notices precise distinctions, rendering an advantage to the left in the specialised functions of language, causal relationships and fine motor movements. By contrast, the right is better at analysing the global, overall relationship aspects of information. Therefore the right more readily identifies context and gets the overall picture of the situation, giving an advantage to the right hemisphere in processing social interactions, emotional experience and visual-spatial tasks. One metaphor often used is that the left is a digital 'computer' and the right an analogue 'computer'. Another is that the left provides the 'text' and the right the 'context'.

Hemispheric dominance is relative, not absolute. Ornstein (1997) compares this to the 'winner takes all' in politics, where a 51 per cent majority can win the election. Translated into neuroscience this means a hemisphere does not function 100 per cent in its area of speciality, only *relatively* more than the other hemisphere. The left contains some emotional ability and the right some language ability, even if to a lesser degree than their 'speciality'.

The left and right cerebral cortices share their specialised skills by communicating with one another across the corpus callosum. Therefore, in the healthy brain modular lateralised cortical functions are integrated. The emotional processing right side influences what the verbalising left side is aware of, and conversely left-hemisphere linguistic input can influence right hemisphere emotional experience.

The aim in this chapter is to present the data upon which the 'asymmetric but integrated' theory of hemisphere function is built. Evidence is given for the specialised functions of each hemisphere, as well as the evidence for how the two hemispheres function as an integrated whole. Clinical implications are addressed as they relate to the bilateral nature of the brain, such as psychological development, repressive defences, different states of consciousness and the role of language versus non-verbal communication in analysis.

THE RIGHT HEMISPHERE

The right hemisphere is dominant for socio-emotional function-ing, visual-spatial tasks, musical ability, somaesthetic sensation, contextual information and shifts of attention (Joseph, 1988, 1996; Gazzaniga, 1995).

Socio-emotional information and non-verbal communication

Right-hemisphere superiority for emotion includes perception, expression and memory of social and emotional information. Right-hemisphere dominance for emotion is related to its bilateral control over the autonomic nervous system and cortisol production, and its greater connectivity to limbic structures (Joseph, 1988; Wittling & Pfluger, 1990; Schore, 1994). The right hemisphere control over global shifts of attention (Tucker, 1981) is probably important in the regulation of affect states. Dominance over social and emotional processing explains why the right hemisphere is specialised for face recognition and identification of emotional expressions of the face, as well as why the left half of the face is more expressive of emotion (Moreno et al., 1990).

Related to its socio-emotional dominance, the right hemisphere is superior for non-verbal prosodic elements of speech, including rate, inflection, pitch, timbre and melody of vocal expression. Human vocal prosody probably evolved from animal vocalisations. It con-tributes emotion and intent to spoken language and is crucial to the 'meanings' of verbal exchange (Tucker et al., 1977). Prosody is why we detect the emotions and intentions of the speaker even if they are speaking a foreign language and why *pre-verbal* infants infer emotion from the speech of caretakers (Fernald, 1993). Specialisation for prosody, emotion and context explains why the right hemisphere is better at processing jokes, since this depends on non-verbal inflections, facial expression and the overall intent of what is being said.

Musical ability

Musical ability is localised on the right, perhaps because music involves *relationships between* sounds and like emotion, music is expressed in pitch, timbre and frequency. Musicians who suffer right-hemisphere damage develop *amusia*, the inability to recognise familiar melodies and to play them (Luria, 1973). Despite significant aphasia, patients with left-hemisphere damage retain the ability to sing. Not only music, but all non-verbal and environmental sounds are better processed by the right hemisphere, including water splashing, wind blowing and door banging (Joseph, 1993, 1996).

Visual-spatial ability

The right hemisphere is superior for perception and analysis of visual space including depth, distance, direction, orientation and perspective. Therefore it is considered the 'artistic' side of the brain (Gazzaniga, 1995; Joseph, 1996). The right is better at detecting contextual information such as figure-ground relationships, and perceiving whole objects from incomplete sensory information,

such as a cup partly obscured by a milk carton. The right is also
better at finding the correct route, learning mazes and determining
the positional orientation of the body and body parts. Therefore the
right hemisphere allows us to orient ourselves in space, find our
way without getting lost, and in general 'see the wood for the trees'.

Somaesthetic sensation and body image

The right *parietal* lobe processes *somaesthetic* sensation. These
sensations include light touch, pressure, temperature, pain, vibra-
tion, overall body position and position of individual joints. Sensory
input from each side of the body, such as vision and hearing, is generally processed by the *contralateral* hemisphere. However, for
somaesthetic sensation, parietal cortex on the right is sensitive to
input from *both* sides of the body, though more so on the left. As a
result the right hemisphere is intimately involved in representations of the body and body image.

Right-hemisphere damage

Frontal lobe damage, particularly on the right, causes deficits in
socio-emotional functioning. Such patients show inappropriate social
behaviour and emotional expression. They often speak in monotone
and lose the ability to express or detect the social and emotional cues
embedded in spoken conversation (Kaplan et al., 1990). Although
they comprehend words, sentences and paragraphs, they fail to

grasp the appropriate context, emotional significance and overall intent of the speaker. These patients are rather concrete and literal. When asked to interpret the meaning of 'He has a heavy heart', they are more likely to select a picture of a person staggering under the weight of a big heart, rather than a picture of someone crying.

Damage that includes the right *parietal* lobe can result in two strange clinical conditions related to body representation, 'hemineglect' and 'anosognosia' (Greek for no knowledge of disease). These conditions are postulated to be the result of deficits of awareness and feedback of somaesthetic sensation (Damasio, 1994; Ramachandran et al., 1997; Turnbull, 1997). Patients with a right-hemisphere stroke, who have *anosognosia*, although paralysed on the left side of their body, deny their disability. Patients with paralysis in the left leg report that they can walk 'just fine'. Despite paralysis in the left arm, they exclaim they can lift with the arm 'perfectly well'. One patient, when asked to move her paralysed left arm, would look at the inert limb and say, 'I can see "it" doesn't seem to want to do much by itself'. This illustrates that in addition to 'denial of illness', these patients may fail to acknowledge the damaged limb as their own. They may be startled by its appearance in the bed, saying something like, 'What is my brother's arm doing here?' Patients with right-hemisphere stroke who have *hemineglect* fail to attend to, respond to or recall sensory information presented to the left half of their face and body. They may fail to comb their hair, or brush their teeth on the left. They may eat only from the right side of their plate, read only the right side of the page and if presented with a word such as *toothpaste* they may 'see' only the word *paste*.

Despite rather obvious impairments the patients themselves appear emotionally indifferent to their deficits. As a result of denial of illness and lack of concern, they often make inappropriate plans regarding their future. Supreme Court Justice William O. Douglas, after a right-hemisphere stroke renders him paralysed and wheel-chair bound, leaves the hospital against medical advice, returns to work at his office, and is reported to boast that any news of his paralysis is a myth! Paradoxically, while these patients deny disability, they may at the same time personify an affected limb. They may call it insulting names, such as 'the nuisance' or develop an intense hatred of the impaired limb and physically abuse it.

Research by Adolphs and others supports the widely held notion that the right hemisphere is specialised for processing emotion. Their work with brain-damaged patients further suggests that the recognition of emotional facial expressions is impaired with damage to the right parietal or right mesial occipital lobe. These patients have most difficulty recognising fear, and to some degree other negative emotions. Patients with left-hemisphere damage show no impairment in recognising any facial expression of emotion. These findings are consistent with a view that the right hemisphere may be more involved with negative as opposed to positive emotions.

THE LEFT HEMISPHERE

The left hemisphere processes information as discrete units in a linear sequential time frame. Since fine motor control requires precisely co-ordinated muscle contractions and language depends on linear sequencing, it is assumed that left-hemisphere superiority for temporal sequencing is the basis for its dominance for handedness and linguistic functioning (Joseph, 1996; Miller et al., 1993).

Fine motor control

In the majority of people the left hemisphere is dominant for fine motor control of fingers, hands and arms, which is why most people are right-handed. While the *right* hemisphere better locates an object in space and solves manipulo-spatial problems such as aiming, it is the *left* hemisphere that is responsible for *accurate* throwing. This is because the accuracy of the throw requires a series of linearly sequenced motor contractions in the throwing arm, hand and fingers. The left hemisphere is also dominant for fine motor control over the articulatory 'speech' muscles of mouth, tongue and pharynx. From Calvin's (1993) evolutionary perspective, speech involves the precise and accurate 'throwing' of words. He theorises that linear sequencing of language is built on the same neural circuitry that is responsible for the accurate throwing needed to hunt game.

Dominance for language

Left-hemisphere dominance for language exists in over 80 per cent of right-handers and 50 per cent of left-handers. Therefore for

a majority of humans, the left hemisphere mediates linguistic functioning, including all aspects of receptive and expressive speech,
reading, writing, spelling, and naming. It is also dominant for
grammar, syntax, verbal concept formation, verbal memory, analytic reasoning. Most likely the left hemisphere is associated with
those aspects of consciousness dependent on language.

Language development

While the left hemisphere eventually dominates over linguistic
functions, the *development* of language reveals the important role
played by the right. The right hemisphere matures before the left
(Chiron et al., 1997). From birth to 3 months, vocal expression
involves purely reflexive vocalisations under the influence of subcortical limbic and brainstem structures (Meltzoff, 1990). By 3–4
months, the 'early babbling' stage, the orbitofrontal cortex, particularly on the right, begins to mature and gain control over the limbic
system. In this way reflexive vocalisations are linked with specific
emotional states and take on emotional meaning (Joseph, 1982;
Scheibel, 1991). The first words, such as 'no', are most probably due
to right-hemisphere activity.

Although the left hemisphere does not significantly begin to
mature until about 18 months, by 4 months there is evidence of
increasing dendritic growth on the left (Scheibel, 1991). This corresponds to the 'late babbling' stage, when infants begin to respond
to specific speech sounds and their phonemic characteristics. The
left hemisphere places a temporal sequential 'stamp' on speech

sounds and the accompanying prosodic expression of pitch, melody and contour.

High levels of circulating testosterone in the perinatal period slow maturation of the left hemisphere, and the left hemisphere is more susceptible to damage from anoxia. Therefore even healthy boys, and infants of either gender with perinatal complications, are slower to develop language and more prone to learning disabilities.

Although not all neuroscientists agree, Joseph (1996) proposes an intriguing theory relating the 'egocentric speech' of children to maturation of the corpus callosum. Callosal maturation begins at approximately 18 months and continues until about 6–8 years. Joseph theorises that the child of 3–4 years of age is thinking out loud, commenting on and describing its actions. Although others may be present, the child is talking to itself. Joseph suggests that before the corpus callosum fully matures, activity in the dominant right hemisphere is not completely available to the left hemisphere. By verbalising its actions to itself, the child's left hemisphere gains 'external' access to behaviours planned, initiated and mediated by the right, and re-encodes them as temporally sequenced information. Once the corpus callosum matures, the transfer of information from right to left occurs internally. Remnants of 'out loud' right to left hemisphere communication are retained. Consider the comment usually ascribed to E. M. Forster; 'I don't know what I think, until I hear what I say'.

Three regions on the left are most often associated with language function. Wernicke's region is an auditory association area in the superior temporal lobe. The inferior parietal lobule (IPL) is a multimodal association area at the junction of the temporal, parietal and occipital lobes. Broca's area in the frontal lobe is involved in 'premotor' aspects of speech. These regions form a 'language axis' and are highly connected with one another, as well as with other brain regions.

Auditory cortex processes all sounds in a simultaneous parallel manner. To comprehend speech, Wernicke's area separates speech sounds into distinct but interrelated phonemes, words and sentences and sequences them in a temporal order. Damage to Wernicke's area causes receptive aphasia, in which speech sounds are a blur of parallel auditory input. 'Big black dog' may sound like 'blickbakgod'. Wernicke's aphasics can speak, but often show word and sound substitutions, neologisms and non sequiturs. They are sometimes unaware of the abnormalities of their speech, since due to Wernicke's damage, they cannot comprehend that what they say is meaningless (Maher et al., 1994). Originally conceptualised as purely *receptive*, Wernicke's aphasia also contains problems with verbal *expression*, presumably because what we plan to say involves the same mechanisms that decode what we hear. Since Wernicke's aphasia results from left-hemisphere damage, patients retain the ability to understand emotional commands and questions, a right-hemisphere mediated function. They may properly respond to 'How are you?' (i.e. they say 'fine!'). However, if one asks, 'Is it raining today?' with the same tone of voice as one uses with 'How are you?', the patient still will say 'fine!'

The IPL is an association area, where integrated polymodal sensory information, such as tactile, proprioceptive and visual, is organised into linear sequence. The IPL and Wernicke's are highly interconnected and their information well integrated. To illustrate how the language axis might operate, if a verbal reply to a question is required, the potential contents of the reply are integrated as multimodal information in the IPL and Wernicke's. This information is directed to Broca's region in the frontal 'premotor' area, which organises the motor sequences that underlie verbal utterances.

Damage to Broca's region causes 'expressive' aphasia. Speaking is impaired but language comprehension remains intact. Broca's aphasics show deficits of syntax, grammar and motor output of speaking. While these patients are severely limited in their ability to speak, they may still be able to sing words they cannot say and communicate their emotions, because the right hemisphere remains intact (Joseph, 1988). It is postulated that the right hand is more involved with pointing, waving goodbye and throwing a kiss, because Broca's area is highly interconnected with motor areas responsible for hand and mouth movements (Joseph, 1982).

Signs of Broca's region exist in the fossil record perhaps as far back as *homo habilis*, about two million years ago and perhaps even further back in Australopithecus. This suggests that primitive human ancestors may have had some capacity for speech. Deacon (1997), an evolutionary biologist, proposes that early language was a combination of gesture and guttural vocalisations. However, the brain and vocal tract structures that enable *highly symbolic* and *well articulated* language only emerged approximately 100,000 years ago with the appearance of the first *modern homo sapiens*, Cro Magnon.

Pinker (see Pinker & Bloom, 1990), an adherent of the distinguished linguist Chomsky, believes the human ability to perform complex grammatical and syntactical operations at the tender age of 2–3 years is the result of *innate* grammatical rules, genetically programmed in a grammar module in the left hemisphere. Deacon disagrees. He believes very young children *acquire* grammatical rules by exposure to the numerous examples of them that exist in their native language. He argues that a child's brain is uniquely designed, not with any innate rules of grammar, but with an immature ability for symbolic representation. It is exactly this immaturity that results in the highly generalised symbolic processing necessary to grasp immediately the grammatical and syntactical relationships of whatever language the child is exposed to before the age of 3 or 4. Once a brain matures and consequently develops greater precision of symbolic representation, grammatical and syntactical relationships become more opaque. This is why adults have to learn a new grammar and cannot automatically acquire it. Superiority for temporal sequencing (not a genetic programme!) biases grammar and syntax (linear processes) to become localised on the left as the child acquires its language. Deacon's view is supported by cases of significant left-hemisphere damage early in life, in which the child still develops almost completely normal language capacity in the *right* hemisphere. Deacon's view is aligned with other neuroscience findings that the brain develops largely in relation to experience (see the more detailed discussion of 'experience-dependent' brain development in Chapter 2).

It is advantageous for the brain to process competing operations, such as the linear sequence of individual speech sounds, and the overall emotional intent of the conversation, in separate regions that can 'cross talk' with one another across the corpus callosum.

However, Deacon believes the right is not the *non*-language hemisphere, but is critically involved in language processing at all levels.
Agha (1993) supports Deacon's idea. His linguistic research suggests that the non-linear right hemisphere plays more of a critical
role than previously thought, in a number of the world's languages.
For example, in the Tibetan language, linguistic meaning relies
heavily on the context of the conversation and social cues, both
right-hemisphere functions. Who is present in the room and what
their social hierarchical position in the community is are more pow-
erful indicators of the meaning of words than are syntactical rules.

Ornstein (1997) provides another shift away from a strict 'lateralised' notion of language function. Japanese has a pictograph
alphabet, *kanji*, and a phonetic one, *kana*. Research studies of native
Japanese speakers with brain lesions show that *kana* is processed
better on the left, since phonemes depend on linear organisation
and *kanji* is better handled on the right, since pictographs depend
on overall relationships.

Ornstein provides a fascinating theory relating bilaterality and
written language. Arabic and Hebrew derive from a common
ancient *phonemic* alphabet with the text moving from right to left.
Early *phonemic* alphabets only contained consonants. Vowel sounds
were worked out by the reader from the context. This is equivalent
to distinguishing 'hd n th blk' as *head on the block* verses *hid in the
black* based on context. He argues that it was advantageous for text
to appear first to the left visual field, because the right hemisphere
is superior for context. The Greeks introduced a *phonetic* alphabet
with vowels. Thus words included vowels. Therefore it became
advantageous for text to be written left to right, so that the linear

sequence of which vowel follows the consonant (thus affecting pro-
nunciation of the consonant) first appears to the right visual field,
i.e. the left hemisphere. In fact there was a transitional period in
which Greek text was written, 'as the ox ploughs', meaning alterna-
tively from right to left and left to right. Finally the left to right
direction was settled upon about 550 BC.

'SPLIT BRAIN': PHYSICAL AND FUNCTIONAL

Much understanding of the bilateral nature of the brain derives
from pioneering work by Gazzaniga and Sperry in the 1960s. They
studied patients in whom the fibre tracts (corpus callosum and commisures) that connect the right and left cortices are surgically cut
for the treatment of intractable epilepsy, leaving the two hemispheres essentially disconnected from one another (Gazzaniga,
1992, 1995; Ornstein, 1997). What startled scientists most about
these 'split-brain' patients is that information presented to one half
of the brain can lie completely outside the conscious awareness of
the other half, and each hemisphere can behave independently of
the other. A series of intriguing experiments with 'split-brain'
patients who possess at least some language capacity in their right
hemisphere illustrates these points. In one experiment an object
(let's say a brush) is placed exclusively in the patient's left hand
(right hemisphere), but out of view. When asked, the patient will be
unable to report verbally what the object is, because the left hemisphere is unaware of the object. If the object is placed in full view
along with a series of other objects, the patient can easily *point* to the

correct object (a brush) with the left hand, because the right hemi-sphere 'knows' what the object is. In another experiment, the patient is visually shown two pictures, one picture presented exclu-sively to the right visual field (left hemisphere) and one to the left visual field (right hemisphere). The left hemisphere is shown a *chicken claw* and the right hemisphere a *snow scene*. The patient is then asked to select, from an array of objects placed in full view, the ones associated with the picture they were aware of seeing. The patient will select a picture of a chicken with the right hand, but a picture of a shovel with the left hand. When asked the reason for selecting these two pictures, a chicken and a shovel, the patient might reply, 'Well, the chicken goes with the claw and the shovel is used to clean out the chicken shed'.

Gazzaniga considers that the left brain acts as an 'interpreter' of information, capable of logical deductive reasoning and causal rela-tionships. In fact it appears as if the left hemisphere *continually* and *automatically* assigns causal meanings to the stimuli it receives. In the experiment just described, the left hemisphere is not aware of the snow scene, but is aware of the claw and shovel. The left arrives at a plausible *causal* explanation for claw and shovel. Other experi-ments illustrate how the left hemisphere automatically 'interprets' the reason for an emotional or behavioural response activated by the right hemisphere, even if the left is completely unaware of the stimulus instigator of that response. If the command 'walk!' is flashed exclusively to the right hemisphere, the patient immediately gets up and walks. When questioned as to the reason for walking, the patient's left hemisphere answers, for example, 'I'm going to the cafeteria to get a coke!' In another experiment, a film is shown to the right hemisphere depicting a violent scene. When asked what she had seen, one woman patient replied, 'I don't really know. It was a blur. But I feel scared. Maybe it is this room, or maybe your experiments have me feeling nervous'. Gazzaniga theorises that although the surgically separated left hemisphere is not directly privy to information processed on the right, the patient's resulting behaviour or emotion is experienced by the left and explained by the left, albeit inaccurately. Whereas the right hemisphere is superior to the left in emotion, it is rather poor at making even simple causal inferences. For example, when presented with the words *pin* and *finger* the right hemisphere can select words lexically associated to these (needle, thumb), but only the left hemisphere can make the causal inference and select the word *bleed*. The left hemisphere is constantly, almost reflexively, labelling experiences and giving causal explanations.

But psychoanalytic patients do not suffer a *physical* disconnection between their left and right hemispheres. Use of the Wada test sheds light on what might be considered a *functional* disconnection between the right and left (Risse & Gazzaniga, 1979). In the Wada test normal individuals are injected with sodium amytal into the left carotid artery, rendering the left hemisphere unconscious and the right side of the body paralysed and anaesthetised. The patient's left hand is given an object to palpate, underneath a cloth so the patient cannot see it. When the amytal wears off, the left hemisphere 'wakes up'. The patient is questioned as to what the object was. They typically say, 'I don't know', and even refuse to guess. However, the right hemisphere, with its excellent tactile and somaesthetic capability, can easily 'recognise' the object. Therefore if asked to select, by *pointing*, from a group of objects in full view, they immediately point to the correct object with their left hand. Afterwards they generally say, 'Oh now I remember!', and can accurately name the object. Gazzaniga explains that each hemisphere perceives and stores the kind of information it is best at handling. The left is responsible for encoding verbal information and the right is responsible for emotional, visual-spatial and somaesthetic information. Under normal circumstances, information is freely transmitted between the hemispheres. Based on the results of the Wada test, Gazzaniga postulates that the memory of the palpated object is lateralised to the right side during the period that the left side is 'unconscious'. When the left regains consciousness it still has no access to the right sided information encoded with 'right sided' mechanisms. However, when the right hemisphere 'points' to the correct object, this reactivates the encoded information. The information is then transferred to the left, reprocessed by 'left sided' temporal sequential mechanisms and thus verbalised.

Joseph (1996) uses the results of the Wada test to speculate about 'repressed' memories. Hyper-arousal of trauma functionally inactivates the left hemisphere. As a result, the emotional memory of the trauma is encoded primarily on the right. This information is not available to the left once the trauma is over and the left returns to normal activity. If the left side does not have the information, the person acts as if they don't know the information. Subsequently, if an environmental stimulus triggers reactivation of the right sided memory, the left reprocesses it and the information is verbally 'recalled'.

'Split-brain' patients exhibit a number of odd symptoms due to conflict between the two hemispheres. One patient experiences difficulty shopping. The right hand puts an item in the cart and the left takes it back out. Another patient complains that when they button up their shirt with their right hand, the left hand immediately unbuttons it. Yet another patient often strikes his wife with his left hand, much to the embarrassment of his left (speaking) hemisphere.

MATURATION OF RIGHT VERSUS LEFT HEMISPHERE

The prefrontal cortex performs the 'executive functions' of the brain—the ability to regulate emotion, anticipate and plan for the future, make rational decisions and shape behaviour towards attainment of motivational goals. Psychological development, in neuroscience terms, is maturation of the prefrontal cortex. Maturation is a measure of growth of circuits, synaptogenesis and myelinisation of neurons (Chiron et al., 1997). The right hemisphere, including the prefrontal region, begins to mature earlier than the left. At approximately 18 months a shift occurs and the left hemisphere begins to mature. This coincides with the emergence of spoken language and the onset of myelinisation of the corpus callosum.

Of particular importance to psychoanalysis is the maturation, on the right, of the orbitofrontal region of the prefrontal cortex during the first year and a half of life. This is because the orbitofrontal region is the seat of emotional self-regulation. Schore (1994, 1997), as a result of his analysis of research data from a vast number of neuroscientists, has formulated a very detailed theory of how orbitofrontal maturation occurs in stages and is dependent on emotion-laden interactions between the infant and its caretakers. He proposes that ultimately the orbitofrontal cortex subserves the self-regulation of affect states. Prior to 3 months of age, emotion is mediated by *subcortical* limbic structures such as the amygdala. According to Schore's account, starting about 3 months of age the onset of orbitofrontal cortex maturation is heralded by the emergence of smiling exchanges between mother and infant. These affect-laden interactions stimulate myelinisation of neural circuits that connect visual cortex with orbitofrontal cortex.

At about 6 to 9 months, the *multimodal* (including vocalisation, body movement, smiling, and eye contact) high-intensity positive affect exchanges that occur between mother and infant, specifically stimulate growth of *dopaminergic* circuits. Dopaminergic circuits subserve the infant's ability to sustain the high levels of sympathetic nervous system arousal that can be considered as the neural basis of emotional excitement and joy. At approximately 10–12 months, growth of the dopaminergic circuits ushers in a period of high positive affect. During this phase parents begin to inhibit their child's behaviour and say 'no'. This inhibitory input stimulates growth of *noradrenergic* circuits. These noradrenergic circuits regulate parasympathetic nervous system activity to decrease arousal and excitement and can be considered as the neural substrate of the emotion of shame (for more description of the relationship between sympathetic and parasympathetic nervous system see Chapter 4). Activity of dopaminergic and noradrenergic circuits is initially dependent on the caretaker as *external* regulator. When mature, these circuits serve as the infant's *internal* self-regulatory system. Growth of these circuits links the right orbitofrontal cortex with subcortical limbic circuits, which is why the right orbitofrontal cortex retains dominance over emotional non-verbal processes for the life of the individual.

At about 18 months, maturation switches from right hemisphere to left. At the same time, *within* the prefrontal cortex, maturation shifts from orbitofrontal to *dorsolateral* prefrontal cortex. Maturing circuits now link dorsolateral prefrontal cortex with *non*-limbic regions of the brain such as the inferior parietal lobule (Tucker, 1992). Dorsolateral development, more on the left than right, corresponds with the onset of language and increasing *non*-emotional executive functions, such as the ability to hold in mind sensory information during periods of distraction. While the orbitofrontal region, particularly on the right, is linked with expression and regulation of emotion, the dorsolateral region, particularly on the left, is linked with abstract thinking skills.

LATERAL VERSUS BILATERAL CONTROL OF EMOTION

The role of the frontal lobes in emotional behaviour is well documented (Dawson & Fischer, 1994). The frontal lobes are asymmetrical with regard to emotion, with the right generally considered dominant. For example, an increase in *right* frontal activity occurs when infants are separated from their mother, or when adults respond negatively to a movie. However, a fair amount of evidence suggests the asymmetrical division may not be as clear-cut as once believed.

The common assumption has been that the right hemisphere is superior for *perception* of emotion. Spence et al. (1996) dispute this. Their experiments demonstrate that the left, as well as the right, can accurately perceive and label the emotional *content* of stimuli. However, only the right hemisphere can generate an *autonomic response* to those emotional stimuli. They conclude that right hemisphere superiority for emotion is due to its dominant control over the physiological aspects of emotional responses.

More and more research supports an important role for the left hemisphere in emotion (Dawson & Fischer, 1994). One approach considers *valence* of emotion to be lateralised, with negative emotion on the right and positive emotion on the left. Schore (1994) argues that intensity of emotion is lateralised, with high intensity affects on the right and more moderate intensity affects on the left. Dawson & Fischer believe that evidence by Davidson (Davidson et al., 1990) and Fox (1991) demonstrates that asymmetry of emotional activation reflects an *approach–avoidance* distinction, with the right frontal lobe more involved in 'withdrawal' affects (sadness, disgust, distress) and the left frontal lobe more in 'approach towards' affect states (joy, interest, anger). *Intensity* of emotion, of whatever valence, is associated with generalised activation of *both* left and right. Dawson & Fischer theorise that each half of the frontal lobe uses a different strategy for self-regulation of emotion. The left frontal region relies on sequential strategies, such as language, while the right uses strategies such as attention to novelty and gaze interactions. Dawson & Fischer's argument might be summarised as the right hemisphere is more 'plugged in' to the somatic aspects of emotion and the left is more 'plugged in' to the language aspects of emotion.

Dawson & Fischer apply their work to the issue of innate temperament. Infants who are more likely to cry when separated from mother have higher 'inborn' frontal activity on the right than left, even during 'resting' conditions. Baseline right frontal asymmetry may reflect an innate biological tendency ('temperament') to respond with negative emotion in stressful situations.

Dawson & Fischer are also interested in the relation between frontal lobe asymmetry for emotion and the attachment process. In a series of studies they compare frontal lobe activity in infants of non-depressed mothers with infants of depressed mothers. Non-depressed mothers who play the game 'peekaboo', elicit *left* frontal activity in the infant. When non-depressed mothers leave their babies it elicits *right* frontal activation and signs of distress in the infant. By contrast, when depressed mothers play the game 'peekaboo', their infants exhibit *equal* activation of both hemispheres. When infants are separated from depressed mothers they exhibit a relative rise in *left* frontal activity and fewer signs of distress. They hypothesise that alteration of the 'normal' asymmetric pattern for affect may underlie the clinical finding of avoidant attachment and may predispose these children to later clinical pathology.

BILATERALITY AND SCHIZOPHRENIA

Rotenberg (1994) proposes that schizophrenia results from functional insufficiency of the right hemisphere, perhaps from early emotional experiences in combination with subtle brain damage. He argues there is compensatory *hyper*activity of the left hemisphere. In this model, right hemisphere *hypo*activity leads to the negative symptoms of schizophrenia, including disturbances of attention, distortion of self image, deficits in social relating, affect blunting and concreteness of thinking. In the absence of adequate right sided processing, compensatory *hyper*activity on the left leads to the causal explanations for stimuli that result in delusions. Since the dopaminergic system is more active on the left than the right, medications which reduce dopamine will improve symptoms related to left sided hyperactivity, but will have little effect on negative symptoms. Support for this theory comes from the fact that in schizophrenic patients there is often increased blood flow and metabolic activity on the left hemisphere and reduced blood flow and metabolism on the right.

CONCLUSION AND CLINICAL IMPLICATIONS

Analysts are eager to deepen their understanding of the mind. In the 'decade of the brain' this involves opening up to the possibility that neuroscience can help explain clinical phenomena. Kandel (1998) provides an optimistic outlook when he postulates that talking with patients may actually alter gene expression, providing a window into the way the learning that occurs in analysis may alter emotional and behavioural functioning. However, neuroscientists caution against over-zealous attempts to make specific correlations between psychoanalytic theory and observation with neuroscience ones. We are not *yet* at the point where direct 'translations' can be made between the two fields. We need to learn what neuroscience has to offer, but we also need to understand that, at this point in time, neuroscientific explanations of analytic theory and treatment can only be provisional and tentative.

An important clinical implication follows from the neuroscience perspective that comprehension of the world around us depends on the integrated function of both hemispheres. The right hemisphere 'knows' through grasping the emotion, intent and background context of what is expressed, and can do so outside of conscious awareness. The left contributes linguistic and causal understanding, both of which occur consciously. What this implies for psychoanalysis is that treatment needs to include attention to the (often unconscious) non-verbal emotional cues communicated between patient and analyst, as well as the verbal content of the session. Not only are both equally important but, as the scientific data suggests, words and feelings *mutually interact* to enhance the processing of each. Access to emotion enhances the ability to arrive at linguistic meanings of experience, and putting feelings into words enhances affect regulation.

The work of Dawson & Fischer helps explain two commonly observed clinical phenomena. A patient's ability to put feelings into words (a left-hemisphere strategy), often aids in diminishing the intensity of painful affects. When a patient switches attention to a new subject matter (a right-hemisphere strategy), he may be attempting to decrease painful affects.

One of the more intriguing scientific findings to theorise about as to clinical relevance, is the lateralised left hemisphere 'interpreter' function. The left hemisphere continually arrives at interpretive meanings and causes for the information it receives, whether it be the external sensory data of environmental stimuli or internal sensory data of emotion and body sensation. Both patient and analyst continually and automatically generate theories and explanations for feelings, behaviours and the contents of verbal interaction. Rationalising defences are perhaps a left-hemisphere function. The humbling factor is that the left hemisphere takes the data available and draws inferences and causal explanations that feel accurate, but may not be. This is why we as analysts, even when we feel we are 'right' about a patient, need to remain open to the fact that our conclusions may be faulty. Perhaps paradoxically, the 'interpreter' function suggests that 'reconstructions' or 'co-constructions of narrative' may be useful in containing a patient's affect even if they do not have exact historical truth.

It must be recognised that at this point in time any attempt to explain psychoanalytic concepts in terms of neurobiology is fraught with conceptual problems and can only be highly speculative. A major reason is that these two fields operate in such different theoretical domains that the terminology cannot be directly translated from one to the other. Keeping this caveat in mind, I offer a few examples of how neuroscience and psychoanalysis might be integrated which may nevertheless be of interest to the reader.

The functional disconnection that occurs between right and left hemisphere has been used to explain a number of clinically relevant issues. The findings of the Wada test suggest that when information is sequestered in the right hemisphere and not available to the talking left hemisphere, an individual is not only unable to speak about the information but may also be unconscious of the information. As mentioned earlier, Joseph (1996) uses these findings to support the concept of 'repressed memory', with the memory of the trauma sequestered in the right hemisphere. Henry (1993) believes that a deficit in interhemispheric transfer results from impairments in the corticosteroid and catecholamine hormonal systems during stress. This leads to the failure to sufficiently process right-hemisphere distress affects in left-hemisphere linguistic terms. As a consequence the patient may develop alexithymia, the inability to put feelings into words. Levin (1997) theorises that certain defences result from functional disconnections between the right and left hemisphere. A disconnection from right to left leads to repression, in which emotion-laden experiences cannot be adequately verbalised. A functional disconnection from left to right leads to disavowal. Patients can speak about emotional events but deny their emotional significance.

Levin (1997) and Modell (1997) believe that the use of metaphor can enhance the integrated function of the right and left hemisphere. By containing within them sensory, imagistic, emotional and verbal elements, metaphors are believed to activate multiple brain centres simultaneously. A failure to integrate right and left hemisphere might also underlie the common clinical phenomena in which patients intellectually 'know' they *must* be having certain feelings, such as sadness or anger over a loss, but cannot consciously access any 'felt' experience of emotion. From a developmental perspective, although the right hemisphere develops prior to the left it is assumed most right-sided information gets re-encoded by the later maturing left. It is postulated however that some does not. Thus some very early affective experiences may remain inchoate and impossible to verbalise.

The neuroscience emphasis on integration of brain function suggests that theoretical debates over what is more 'fundamental' to the analytic process are essentially dead ends. Affect attunement, causal interpretation, understanding of meanings, even perhaps subjectivity and objectivity may all be required, in order to understand the patient's unconscious longings, conflicts and beliefs and to modify the patient's defences.

REFERENCES

AGHA, A. (1993). Structural form and utterance context in Lhasa Tibetan. *Monographs in Linguistics and the Philosophy of Language*. New York: Peter Lang.

CALVIN, W. H. (1993). The unitary hypothesis: a common neural circuitry for novel manipulations, language, plan-ahead, and throwing? In *Tools, Language and Cognition in Human Evolution*. Cambridge: Cambridge Univ. Press, pp. 230–249.

CHIRON, C. ET AL. (1997). The right brain hemisphere is dominant in human infants. *Brain*, 120: 1057–1065.

DAMASIO, A. R. (1994). *Descartes' Error*. New York: Putnam.

DAVIDSON, R. J. ET AL. (1990). Approach withdrawal and cerebral asymmetry: emotional expression and brain physiology. *J. Personality Soc. Psychol.*, 58: 330–341.

DAWSON, G. & FISCHER, K. W. (EDS) (1994). *Human Behavior and the Developing Brain*. New York: Guilford.

DEACON, T. W. (1997). *The Symbolic Species*. New York: Norton.

FERNALD, A. (1993). Approval and disapproval: infant responsiveness to vocal affect in familiar and unfamiliar languages. *Child Devel.*, 64: 657–674.

FOX, N. A. (1991). If it's not the left, it's the right: electroencepha-lograph asymmetry and the development of emotion. *Amer. Psychol.*, 46: 863–872.

GALIN, D. (1974). Lateral specialization and psychiatric issues: Speculation on development and the evolution of consciousness. *Annals New York Acad. Sci.*, 299: 397–411.

GAZZANIGA, M. S. (1992). *Nature's Mind.* New York: Basic Books.

—— (1995). Consciousness and the cerebral hemispheres. In *The Cognitive Neurosciences.* Cambridge, MA: MIT Press.

—— ET AL. (1962). Some functional effects of sectioning the cerebral commisures in man. *Proc. Nat. Acad. Sci. USA*, 48: 1765–1769.

HENRY, J. P. (1993). Psychological and physiological responses to stress: the right hemisphere and the hypothalamo-pituitary-ad-renal axis, an inquiry into problems of human bonding. *Physiological & Behav. Sci.*, 28: 369–387.

JOSEPH, R. (1982). The neuropsychology of development: hemi-spheric laterality, limbic language and the origin of thought. *J. Clin. Psychol.*, 44: 3–34.

—— (1988). The right cerebral hemisphere: emotion, music, visu-al-spatial skills, body image, dreams and awareness. *J. Clin. Psychol.*, 44: 770–779.

—— (1993). *The Naked Neuron: Evolution and the Languages of the Body and Brain.* New York: Plenum.

—— (1996). *Neuropsychiatry, Neuropsychology and Clinical Neuro-science.* Baltimore: Williams and Wilkins.

KANDEL, E. R. (1998). A new intellectual framework for psychia-try. *Amer. J. Psychiat.*, 155: 457–469.

KAPLAN, J. A. ET AL. (1990). The effects of right hemisphere damage on the pragmatic interpretation of conversational remarks. *Brain Lang.*, 38: 315–333.

LEVIN, F. (1997). Integrating some mind and brain views of transference: the phenomena. *J. Amer. Psychoanal. Assn.*, 45: 1121–1152.

LURIA, A. (1973). *The Working Brain.* New York: Basic Books.

MAHER, L. M. ET AL (1994). Lack of error awareness in an aphasic patient with relatively preserved auditory comprehension. *Brain Lang.*, 50: 941–946.

MELTZOFF, A. N. (1990). Towards a developmental cognitive science. *Annals New York Acad. Sci.*, 608: 1–37.

MILLER, E. K. ET AL. (1993). Activity of neurons in anterior inferior temporal cortex during a short term memory task. *J. Neurosci.*, 13: 1460–1478.

MODELL, A. (1997). Reflections on metaphors and affects. *Ann. Psychoanal.*, 25: 219–233.

MORENO, C. R. ET AL. (1990). Lateralisation for the expression and perception of facial emotion as a function of age. *Neuropsychologia*, 28: 199–209.

ORNSTEIN, R. (1997). *The Right Mind.* New York: Harcourt Brace.

PINKER, S. J. & BLOOM, P. (1990). Natural language and natural selection. *Behav. & Brain Sci.*, 13: 707–784.

RAMACHANDRAN, W. S. ET AL. (1997). Mirror agnosia. *Procs. Royal Soc. Lond [Biol.]*, 264: 645–647.

RISSE, G. L. & GAZZANIGA, M. S. (1979). Well-kept secrets of the right hemisphere: a carotid amytal study of restricted memory transfer. *Neurology*, 28: 950–953.

ROTENBERG, V. S. (1994). An integrative psychophysiological approach to brain hemisphere functions in schizophrenia. *Neurosci. Behav. Rev.*, 18: 487–495.

SCHEIBEL, A. B. (1991). Some structural and developmental correlates of human speech. In *Brain Maturation and Cognitive Development.* New York: De Gruyter.

SCHORE, A. N. (1994). *Affect Regulation and the Origin of the Self.* Hillsdale, NJ: Lawrence Erlbaum.

—— (1997). Early organization of the nonlinear right brain and development of a predisposition to psychiatric disorders. *Develop. Psychopathol.*, 9: 595–631.

SPENCE, S. ET AL. (1996). The role of the right hemisphere in the physiological and cognitive components of emotional processing. *Psychophysiol.*, 33: 112–122.

TUCKER, D. M. (1981). Lateral brain function, emotion and conceptualization. *Psychol. Bulln.*, 89: 19–46.

—— (1992). Developing emotions and cortical networks. *Minnesota Symposium on Child Psychology: Vol. 24. Developmental Behavioral Neuroscience.* Hillsdale NJ: Erlbaum.

—— ET AL. (1977). Affective discrimination and evocation in patients with right parietal disease. *Neurology*, 27: 947–950.

TURNBULL, O. H. (1997). Mirror, mirror, on the wall—is the left side there at all? *Current Biology*, 7: 709–711.

WITTLING, W. & PFLUGER, M. (1990). Neuroendocrine hemisphere asymmetries: salivary cortisol secretion during lateralised viewing of emotion-related and neutral films. *Brain Cognition*, 14: 243–265.

6: CONSCIOUSNESS:
A NEUROSCIENCE PERSPECTIVE

'Plato said we are trapped inside a cave and know the world only through the shadows it casts on the wall ... The skull is our cave and mental representations the shadows' (Pinker, 1997, p. 84).

INTRODUCTION:
BASIC ASSUMPTIONS OF CONSCIOUSNESS RESEARCH

The majority of consciousness research is steeped in an evolutionary perspective and a fundamental assumption of 'mind–brain unity'. Single-cell organisms do not need brains, because they interface directly with their environment through chemo-tactic receptors. The brain evolved as an information processor, to bring the 'outside inside' so that the whole organism is privy to environmental stimuli. Primitive brains react reflexively. The higher vertebrate brain emerged because natural selection favours brains that respond rapidly, yet are flexible enough to adapt to changing environments.

For neuroscientists, 'mind–brain unity' refers to the way in which the brain encodes information as configurations of electrically activated neural networks. Network patterns function as a kind of Morse code that can represent the world. Networks are built up from individual neurons or groups of neurons (neuronal groups) by the intrinsic properties of nerve tissue. All nerve cells intrinsically generate electrical oscillations, independent of external and internal sensory input, and signal their excitement to neighbouring cells through synaptic connections (Hobson, 1994; Llinas, 1990). Because neurons have so many synaptic connections to other neurons, even small variations of firing in local neuronal groups lead to significant variations of firing within the widely distributed neural networks that underlie complex brain functions.

Because the concept of consciousness is complex, it is studied much like the fabled elephant, in which one wise man touches the ear, another the trunk and another the leg. In parallel fashion, this discussion breaks the subject down into the 'what, how, where, when, why and whence' of consciousness. Following this, the theoretical work of neuroscientists Llinas, Edelman, Tononi and Hobson is presented, since they attempt to integrate the diverse data into a coherent picture. We have chosen to discuss their theories because they address a broad range of the concepts neuroscientists struggle with, and although they disagree on a number of points, there is much overlap and much that is compatible between them.

HISTORICAL AND PHILOSOPHICAL BACKGROUND

'Western thought', influenced by the ideas of Plato and Descartes, has always associated the idea of consciousness with dualistic notions of the mind. There is the rational 'conscious' mind and the irrational 'unconscious' mind, the irrational usually being associated with the 'mythic', or spirits, or the Devil, which induce forbidden wishes, dreams and irrational behaviour. Descartes takes the long-established split between 'divine soul' and 'mortal body' and secularises it to render a duality between 'mind' and 'body', which has become part of our 'common sense', and is difficult for 'Western' cultures to remove from daily thinking. This dualism assumes that there is a 'self' or 'mind' over and against a 'body'. It is inherent in 'traditional' dualism that some kind of central co-ordinator or inner homunculus brings all brain processes together to produce rational conscious thought (Dennett, 1991). Dualism, some might argue, also pervades the thinking of psychoanalytic theorists who separate the conscious mind from the unconscious one.

At the heart of human experience, the question of consciousness has captured the interest of prominent philosophers, who often refer to it as the 'mystery of consciousness' (Churchland, 1996; Searle, 1997). In no other area of neuroscience is the philosophical as intertwined with the scientific. Therefore any discussion of consciousness ought to include at least mention of the major philosophical debates. One debate centres around the question of whether the brain is essentially a computational device. Within this debate there are those who believe that the brain can be likened to a computer, with the brain as the 'hardware' and the mind as the 'software'. They assert that eventually computers will be able to do all that the brain can do. This viewpoint, typified by the philosopher Dennett (1991), is often called strong AI (artificial intelligence). Dennett conceptualises the mind as a 'virtual' machine created out of the neural networks of the brain's 'hardware', similar to the way in which computers can simulate virtual reality for pilots to learn how to fly a plane. Dennett believes that the 'mind' is independent of the 'machine' that creates it, and therefore we can learn little of the mind from the study of anatomy and physiology. The mathematician, physicist and philosopher Penrose (1994) typifies an opposing view. He argues that the human brain is not like a computer, because the mind is too complex to be reducible to the mathematics of computer programmes. He and the philosopher Chalmers (in Searle, 1997) argue that our current science, including computer science, biology, chemistry, even physics, is insufficient to explain consciousness. They believe that eventually a revolutionary advance in the field of physics will be able to explain it.

Another major philosophical debate centres around the idea of mind–brain unity, i.e. mental phenomena are the result of the activity of neurons. On one side of the debate are those, such as Eccles (1989), who find the inherent 'reductionism' in mind–brain unity objectionable. They argue that the 'soul' and other higher human mental functions such as self-reflection cannot be reduced to biology and chemistry. They want to reserve some kind of phenomena beyond the physical to explain these. On the other side of this debate are philosophers such as Searle (1997) and Churchland (1996), who consider consciousness to be an ordinary biological phenomenon comparable to growth, digestion or the secretion of bile. Consciousness is a function of the brain in the way that digestion is a function of the stomach. They strongly believe that neuroscience will eventually be able to explain consciousness completely.

Essentially all neuroscientists reject the idea of a 'mental–physical' dualism. Both Searle and Churchland maintain that eliminating dualism, however, does not mean reducing human experience, such as spiritual feelings or subjective qualities like beauty, to mere ions, molecules and synapses. But their reasons differ. Searle contends that lower-level neuronal processes lead to 'emergent properties' such as consciousness and the private subjective qualities of personal sensory experience (called 'qualia' by philosophers). An 'emergent property' is one that can be causally explained by the behaviour of the elements of a system, but is not a property of any of the individual elements of the system, nor a summation of the properties of the elements. The liquidity of water is an example. The behaviour of the H_2O molecule can explain the liquid state of water, but neither hydrogen nor oxygen are liquids. Churchland believes that Searle's view that physical events *lead* to mental events sidesteps the issue. Churchland believes that the 'physical' and 'mental' cannot be separated, and that physical properties of the brain do not simply *cause* mental states. She argues that electricity is not *caused* by the movement of electrons; it *is* the movement of electrons. Temperature is not *caused* by the mean molecular kinetic energy; it *is* the mean molecular kinetic energy. In a similar fashion, causation and identity of conscious states are one and the same. Churchland believes that our ability to accept that consciousness is a property of the neural processes of the human brain will come in time with greater scientific understanding. According to Olds (1995), process dualism may have a place in thinking about the brain–mind relationship. By process dualism he means that the 'semiotic' processes that convey information in life forms distinguish the living world from the non-living, physical universe. In his model, consciousness is a source of information about brain processes.

Another important debate taken up by philosophers is called 'the binding problem'. While initially 'the binding problem' was identified in relation to perception, it now has expanded to other brain functions such as memory, consciousness and representation in gen-

eral. As well described by Crick (1994), 'the binding problem' refers
to the fact that modular brain areas are specialised for processing
different aspects of sensory experience, such as colour, shape and
spatial location, yet the brain is able to integrate signals that are separated in space and time into a whole unified experience. In object
recognition, the separate modalities of touch, sight and sound are
integrated into whole objects. In conversation, separate phonemes
are integrated into words and into sentences and into whole conversations. In binocular vision, the two separate images from each eye
are integrated into a single visual image. Thus when we see a blue
ball moving diagonally down a ramp, although the brain processes
each feature in a separate modular brain region, we nevertheless 'see'
the whole event, not the blue colour separate from the spherical
shape, separate from the diagonal line of motion. For philosophers
and neuroscientists alike, 'the binding problem' is a central dilemma
that must be explained by any neuroscience theory of consciousness.

THE NATURE OF CONSCIOUSNESS: THE *WHAT?*

There is a growing consensus that whatever consciousness is, it
is not a unitary thing, but is a class of phenomena that includes
several different states, all having in common the general property
of being aware (Mountcastle, 1998). Philosophers and neuroscientists emphasise that understanding 'subjectivity', the experience of
being conscious, is the 'hard' problem in contrast to the 'easy' problem of describing the neurophysiology and neuroanatomy of consciousness (Chalmers, in Searle 1997). Although it is very difficult
for neuroscientists to agree on an exact definition, most use con-

sciousness in the ordinary sense of the word, meaning awareness (Hirst, 1995; Moscovitch, 1995). Consciousness is a psychological or mental phenomenon in which we are aware of perception, of memory, of thought, of action, of self, and of the very process of being conscious.

Consciousness is not an 'all or nothing' phenomenon (Hirst, 1995). There are varying degrees of consciousness; unconsciousness gradates into consciousness; and unconscious mental contents can have an effect on consciousness. Whether a stimulus becomes conscious depends, in part, on the degree of sensory analysis and on one's exact definition of unconscious verses conscious. Using a strict definition, Hirst argues that 'unconscious' applies when stimuli are processed only to a 'shallow' degree or 'low-level'. 'Low-level' analysis includes only the physical attributes of stimuli and most probably involves the primary sensory cortices. These representations are so impoverished they cannot support conscious recognition, but can still influence other mental events. Examples of 'low-level' analysis are the shape of the letters of the word 'bottle', the circles and contours of a face and the spatial location of an object. Hirst proposes that 'primed' memory, implicit learning tasks and 'subliminally' presented stimuli involve only 'low-level' sensory processing and therefore remain fully unconscious in the 'strict sense' (for more on memory, see Chapter 3). These findings are consistent with the work of Shevrin, who proposes that stimuli that involve a paucity of exposure (e.g. 'subliminal' stimuli), although not consciously registered, may in fact 'prime' later thoughts and images that emerge in the clinical situation (Shevrin et al., 1996).

In a less strict definition of unconscious, the 'iffy' 'twilight' area where there is some, albeit very vague, degree of awareness, a more complex or 'deep level' of analysis is involved, most probably involving association cortices. Analysis is considered 'deep' once it involves some degree of identification of objects and their meaning. Bisiach & Berti (1995) discuss 'unconscious' in relation to anosognosia and hemineglect, syndromes that can result from cerebrovascular damage (i.e. stroke) in the right hemisphere, most often in the parietal region. Patients with anosognosia, despite significant paralysis on their left side, deny conscious awareness of their disability. In the case of hemineglect, patients report no conscious awareness of sensory information to the left side of their body. Bisiach & Berti propose that patients with anosognosia and hemineglect are 'unconscious' of disability and stimuli only in this 'less strict' sense. They do evidence that 'twilight' range of at least some level of conscious awareness on certain cognitive tests and physiological responses such as the galvanic skin response or 'GSR' (a measure that reflects skin sweat production). Bisiach & Berti (1995) believe these syndromes suggest that the significant distinction is not between unconscious and conscious at all, but between states of 'co-consciousnesses'. They theorise that the apparent lack of conscious awareness in these syndromes is due to a lack of sufficient integration between dissociated 'co-states' of consciousness. Unlike psychoanalytic theory, neuroscientific paradigms of the unconscious involve 'lower-level' representations that do not involve symbolic meanings. Also that which appears to operate unconsciously might rather be considered a dissociated state of consciousness.

Some neuroscientists consider that desynchronised EEG activity correlates with conscious states (Edelman, 1989; Hobson, 1994; Llinas & Churchland, 1996). From this perspective, since both waking and REM sleep involve dysynchronised EEG activity, waking and dreaming are considered to be alternate states of consciousness, that differ only in the origin of their sensori-motor inputs.

THE PROCESS OF CONSCIOUSNESS: THE *HOW*?

Consciousness is often discussed in relation to the 'a' words, awake, alert, aroused, attentive, aware, self-aware, all of which depend on activation of circuits ascending from the brainstem to the cortex. Because of their wide anatomical distribution and neurochemistry, brainstem systems are able to provide the global activation of the brain necessary for consciousness to occur. The reticular activating system drives arousal. It 'announces' to the brain regions higher up, 'stimulus coming! Get ready!' The locus coeruleus, the major source of brain norepinephrine, contributes to alertness and attention. Activity in the locus coeruleus 'turns on' in the morning to wake us up from sleep. Activation of the cholinergic circuits is necessary for the 'consciousness' of dream sleep.

Attention is necessary for something to reach conscious awareness. Attention implies focus on something, whether an object, sensation, thought or image. While we can pay attention to and be conscious of more than one thing at a time, there are limits. Consciousness cannot hold on to many things at a time. The ability to attend to more than one piece of sensory information depends on how hard it is to keep the two pieces of information segregated. It is easier to hold in consciousness one auditory and one visual message than either two auditory or two visual ones. It is easier to hold in consciousness a list of animal terms and a list of vegetable terms than two lists of either animal terms or vegetable terms.

For events to be consciously perceived, they must be significant to the 'self'. The 'self system' is as essential to consciousness as an intact perceptual system is to perception. One way to conceptualise consciousness is as the interaction of the 'self system' and 'non-self system' (i.e. external world). According to Damasio & Damasio (1996) the 'self system' involves both the invariant activity in neural mechanisms that represent body state, motor actions and relationships, and the changes in those representations in response to sensory stimuli. Because the right hemisphere, more than the left, is connected to somato-sensory information and the autonomic nervous system in both halves of the body, the 'self system' may be more localised in the right brain. The Damasios and others such as Edelman (1989) consider that consciousness involves very rapid shifts back and forth between 'self system' representations and the representations of sensory images.

In a related model by Gray (1995), a central 'comparator', on a moment-to-moment basis, compares the current state of the organism's perceptual world with the predicted state derived from the 'self system'. Most of the time the brain keeps reaffirming that nothing has changed from what would be predicted. When something does change (something moves, or something unexpected happens), the comparator notes a mismatch and that is the instant of consciousness. This theory may have promise, from an analytic point of view. A patient lying on a couch has a rather static visual environment, especially with eyes closed. Because the brain is always look-ing for change, on the couch with so little external distraction it will look for change and follow the change in the stream of thoughts and associations.

A distinction is often made between the content of consciousness and the process that produces it. We are conscious of objects, ideas, meanings, decisions and actions—but not of the brain processes themselves that produce consciousness. There is a tendency, per-haps unfortunate, to conceptualise 'process' and 'content' as a kind of 'container' and 'contained' model. Clearly this distinction is prob-lematic since it is hard to imagine that there could be a container that did not contain anything, or a conscious content with no proc-ess. However, Lakoff & Johnson (1980) contend that although 'con-tainer models' may be conceptually flawed, we are nevertheless somewhat constrained into using them. This is because, as they argue, language and thought derive from bodily experience. For example, we conceptualise feelings as derived from within the body, such as 'the love in my heart'. A strong advocate of the container model, Baars (1996) conceptualises a 'global workspace' in which processes such as attention and short-term memory contain the mental contents of which we are conscious at that moment.

Using the 'process–content' distinction, Solms (1997) elaborates on Freud, and theorises that consciousness is like a sense organ per-ceiving inwardly, a kind of built-in monitor of other brain functions. Solms believes that the contents of consciousness are the data of the senses, the data of memory and the inward appreciation of affects. Solms concludes that the process of consciousness is the same pro-cess that produces sensation and perception, thought and affect.

While they might argue with his 'process–content' distinction, Lli-nas & Edelman, whose work is elaborated on later in this chapter, would agree with Solms that consciousness requires no new neural processes. Consciousness differs only in that it results from more complex integration of the same basic processes that produce other mental phenomena.

THE ANATOMY OF CONSCIOUSNESS: THE *WHERE?*

A number of neurological syndromes initially led neuroscientists to the conclusion that some localised region was the 'seat' of con-sciousness. For a time it was considered the cortex, since damage to the primary (striate) visual cortex leads to loss of conscious aware-ness of visual stimuli. However, rather fascinatingly, unlike a person with damage to the retina, or optic nerve, the 'cortically' blind per-son reports no conscious awareness of seeing anything, but when walking can avoid most obstacles in their path. This condition is known as 'blindsight' and may be the result of the kind of 'low-level' analysis discussed by Hirst (1995).

The syndrome known as 'split brain' arises from a cut in the corpus callosum, which divides the two hemispheres (Gazzaniga et al., 1962). Of interest in the present context are studies in which an object is presented visually to the isolated right hemisphere. When asked to name the object, it is as if the visual stimulus does not enter consciousness, because the patient will say 'I see noth-ing!' At the same time, experiments show that the object is per-ceived and registered at some level. The patient can point to the correct object, and rate feelings about the object, such as liking it or not. In one experiment the picture of a nude man is presented to the isolated right hemisphere of a woman. She says she 'sees' nothing, but at the same time she blushes and giggles. It is assumed the person receives the images up to the level of object recognition in the right temporal 'association' cortex. But transfer into the 'linguistic' left brain is missing. Self-reflective consciousness seems to require that step.

Other syndromes at first glance might also appear to support a localised model of consciousness. A stroke in the parietal cortex of the right hemisphere leads to the unilateral hemineglect syndrome. The patient cannot even conceive of anything of interest on the left side of the body nor in the left half of the visual field. In essence the person is not conscious with regard to the left hemispace. And in the other syndrome caused by right parietal damage, anosognosia, the patient behaves as if not conscious of any paralysis of the left side, stoutly denying that anything is wrong at all.

Even recently, because of the role of the hippocampus in episodic memory, Moscovitch (1995) theorises that it is a kind of 'centre' for consciousness. He believes that all consciously perceived information is automatically processed by the hippocampus and is later recalled as conscious explicit memory (see Chapter 3). He feels that consciousness is a 'feature' of explicit memory, separate from the content. When memory is retrieved, the features of perceptual content are linked with the feature of consciousness. Others disagree with Moscovitch, since the hippocampus is not essential for consciousness. A patient with hippocampal damage or Alzheimer's disease may have memory deficits but is still considered conscious.

These syndromes make it tempting to conclude that there is a special role for 'this, that or the other' brain region in consciousness. However, most neuroscientists today believe that there is no anatomical locus of consciousness, no 'Cartesian Theatre' where 'it all comes together', nor any specialised consciousness centre. Consciousness is not a localised process, but involves the integration of widely distributed modular brain regions. Except for a few types of brain damage, such as to intralaminar nucleii of the thalamus and perhaps to the brainstem, there are few brain lesions that produce a global loss of consciousness (Llinas & Churchland, 1996). Even removal of an entire hemisphere in cases of tumour leaves the patient fully conscious. Kinsbourne (1998) points out that local lesions do not eliminate consciousness. They produce only a limitation on what one can be conscious of. For example, damage to the primary visual cortex eliminates conscious vision and damage to the auditory cortex eliminates conscious hearing. Kinsbourne emphasises that consciousness involves the integration of modular brain regions, and that the specifics of what we are conscious of is always processed in relation to the context of whatever else is happening at the same time. In other words, as he says, conscious 'awareness stands out not by what it is, but by the company it keeps' (1995, p. 1323).

Despite the fact that there is no anatomical location or 'seat of' consciousness, we do subjectively experience that the separate brain functions 'all come together', as a multimodal integration of perceptions. The zebra always has stripes that stay on the zebra and not next to it; and the sound of its hooves comes reliably from its direction.

THE TEMPORAL NATURE OF CONSCIOUSNESS: THE *WHEN?*

In our subjective sense, consciousness appears to be the initiator of behaviour, the decision maker, the centre of will. The work of Libet et al. (1983) suggests otherwise, by revealing that conscious awareness occurs after the fact. Subjectively we experience that first we decide what we want to do and then we act on it. However, in fact the conscious mind is the 'last to know'. For example, the reflex withdrawal from stepping on a tack is followed by consciousness of the act. But Libet's work also demonstrates that even with a voluntary decision to act, an electrical readiness potential in pre-motor areas is detected almost half a second before conscious awareness of the decision. Computations and cogitations leading to the decision to act are initiated first; then later some of them enter the narrow stream of consciousness. Although Libet's experiments demonstrate that subjects are consciously aware of their decision to act shortly after their 'brain' has made the decision, the conscious awareness is registered so quickly that our subjective experience is that we consciously made the choice.

THE FUNCTION OF CONSCIOUSNESS: THE *WHY?*

Some argue that life's tasks could all be done without consciousness, that consciousness is only an 'epi-phenomenon' that 'just happens to accompany' thought and action, and serves no evolutionary adaptation (Gray, 1995; Chalmers, 1996). However, most neuroscientists believe that consciousness evolved as a means by which we can adaptively tailor our responses (Edelman, 1989; Tononi et al.,

1992). With consciousness we selectively choose between a number of response options, as well as inhibit responses already initiated but consciously perceived to be inappropriate to the situation. As an example, we are consciously aware that the person we are talking to says something different from what we anticipated. As we respond, we can change the response already 'cued up' in pre-motor regions, even as we are speaking it. The need to tailor one's behaviour in ways that are not pre-wired reflexes requires self-monitoring of one's own behaviour as quickly as possible. The quickest we become conscious of something is about .5 seconds after the fact—'almost but not quite' instant self-monitoring. Such selective choice and behavioural inhibition most probably involve circuits in the pre-frontal cortex (Knight & Grabowecky, 1995).

Libet's experiments, in which subjects are aware of their decision shortly after they have made it, might appear to aid the 'epi-phe-nomenon' argument. However, consciousness of a decision, although 'after the fact' of decision-making, is adaptive because it occurs 'before the fact' of actual action. Without consciousness, you would have to wait ... until you saw what action you took ... to know what action you had decided to make. This is what appears to occur in 'split-brain' patients, in which the right brain may not be consciously aware of a command to the left hemisphere to take action, for example 'walk!', until they actually get up and walk. Without conscious awareness one would stand a poor chance in a physical contest with a person who is conscious, who knows what he decided to do very quickly after his 'brain' decides, not waiting until his body has moved. Consciousness of decision-making helps 'fine-tune' behavioural responses. For example, in reaching for an object, initial attempts are often not accurate and need fine-tuning as the object is approached. Rather than 'waiting to see' what we did and then 'fine-tune it', conscious awareness of the decision to act lets us quickly know what we 'planned' to do and, when necessary, quickly modify the plan. This feedback system operates as what is called primary consciousness, the awareness of the current continuous stream of perceptual and motor events in 'real time'.

In self-reflective consciousness, the ability to reflect on mental processes including primary consciousness, human beings maintain a kind of 'virtual reality' in which we can make speculations and plans that anticipate changes in the environment. This helps us deal with very rapid and complex changes of human environments. Humphrey (1992) suggests that in the social realm, self-reflective consciousness helps us to predict our own behaviour in order to subject it to the inhibitions necessary for social life; and conscious monitoring of our own emotions helps us to gauge the intentions of others and thereby predict their behaviour.

In so far as consciousness is a form of feedback, it plays a part in a representational or semiotic system (Olds, 1990, 1992, 1995; Deacon, 1997). In this model, in self-reflective consciousness the incoming sense data are re-represented symbolically, and thereby made independent of their source. This creates a 'virtual scene'. An analogy is a video camera. If there is no tape in the camera only a fleeting image occurs, which disappears when the camera is turned off. If there is a videotape recording the input, the scene is preserved, and exists independently of the external reality. It can be replayed, but it can also be edited. Similarly, when we bring memories to consciousness as scenes or in words, this is considered to be symbolic re-representation. Because memory is reconstructed, a representation of an event can be preserved as a 'virtual' scene, but it also can be altered. Herein lies the opportunity for the error and distortion of so-called 'false memory'. But as memory is consciously retrieved and re-worked in therapy, herein also lies the opportunity for change.

THE DEVELOPMENT OF CONSCIOUSNESS: THE *WHENCE?*

It is becoming more apparent that the 'self' and consciousness arise from a dyadic, interpersonal milieu. The infant has many inborn potentials, but they flower only in intense and frequent interactions with the mother and other caretakers. The epigenetic development of mental and physical capacities require time and synchrony with body growth, CNS growth and the attunement of the mother. By implication, conscious awareness of perceptual events, emotional events, social events and aspects of one's own inner life develop over time within a socio-emotional context. Some current developmental theories suggest that the 'sense of self' emerges out of the internalisation of the dyadic relationship with the mother, and that the development of 'self' consciousness emerges as the infant takes the 'self in the dyad' as an object in its inner world.

LLINAS: THE BRAIN AS 'REALITY EMULATOR'

According to the theory proposed by the neuroscientist Llinas (Llinas & Pare, 1996), neural activity of the brain is intrinsically organised to represent the world. The brain has within it pre-formed 'templates' for how to respond to the general outlines of the environment it is expected to live in. Over the animal's lifetime the intrinsic activity is modified in response to the specifics of the ani-mal's actual environment. Llinas, along with neuroscientists such as Edelman, Tononi and Hobson, conceptualises the brain as a 'real-ity emulator'. Despite the subjective experience that we sense the outside world, it is the brain's neural activity patterns that 'simu-late' reality.

The theoretical proposal of Llinas and the others is that the brain operates fundamentally as a closed system. They are not suggesting that the external world has no influence on the brain. Rather, the closed system means that the brain is essentially self-activating, already has intrinsic activity that can represent the world, and that brain neural networks are active even in the absence of inputs from the outside world. The actual sensory inputs and response outputs of an individual serve only to shape and hone the specifics of that intrinsic activity.

In the closed system model, what is proposed is that certain brain capacities such as cognition, while they mature with development and learning, exist *a priori* in the brain at birth as a result of the vicissitudes of evolution. For example, from the very first time light hits the retina, many animals including primates automatically begin to develop a visual world (Weisel & Hubel, 1974). As a result of neural network plasticity, during development there is continu-ing refinement of cognitive images and meanings. As an example, at birth the infant brain can respond to all phonemes. To acquire its native language during development, neural network plasticity leads to enhanced recognition of the phonemes it hears, while the ability to recognise those 'not heard' is lost.

The closed system model emphasises that we do not directly apprehend the outside world. What we do experience is the brain's intrinsic neural activity being modified by sensory inputs. In fact, as we can see from optical illusions such as the Kaniza triangle (see Chapter 2, page 24), the nature of the perception can differ from what is present in the external stimulus. In the closed system model, the dreams that occur during REM sleep are a good example of intrinsic brain activity unmodified by the external environment. Llinas and the others like, perhaps somewhat humorously, to describe waking consciousness as a dream modified by sensory input and motor output. The closed system model may help support psychoanalytic notions of psychic reality. We do not necessarily experience what is actually 'out there'. Rather, the intrinsic design of the brain, along with other intrinsic factors such as evolutionarily determined processing biases, influences what we perceive and what we remember at any given time.

Sensori-motor templates of the environment

The brain evolved a special kind of connectivity within the sensori-motor system so as to enhance the animal's ability to predict changes in the environment on the basis of incoming stimuli and to formulate adaptive responses to that change (Llinas & Pare, 1996; Kinsbourne, 1998). Intrinsic activity is generated in sensory and pre-motor areas, which readies the animal for 'likely' sensory inputs and movement outputs. Llinas theorises that certain neural circuits connecting these areas function as sensori-motor templates. What he means is that sensory perception is automatically connected to the pre-motor areas 'most likely' to be utilised in response to the sensory stimulus (Llinas & Pare, 1996). Reciprocally, motor responses automatically 'tune' sensory areas to sensory inputs most likely to result from that motor response. This enables what Llinas refers to as predictive behavioural interaction, in which a built-in 'anticipatory' system enhances the animal's ability to respond quickly to environmental situations. Llinas's idea is that as we move around the environment we develop simple images of what we will be moving into. When an animal sees a banana, this automatically modifies pre-motor activity to implement motor programmes required for reaching for the banana; and movements to reach for the banana modify sensory activity to 'tune' the visual system to see bananas. Similarly, hearing your friend speak automatically 'cues up' the programmes for words you are 'likely' to use in response. Your response then 'tunes' your hearing for your friend's 'likely' reply. This is why we can sometimes mis-speak. When someone finishes a sentence differently from how we anticipated, we might still blurt out what was already 'cued up' by the automatic sensori-motor template connections.

This linked automatic sensori-motor connectivity helps us to understand the idea of consciousness as a feedback system. Consciousness lets you know what object you have seen, what you decided to do about it, and then by consciously seeing your movement lets you know what action you have taken. At each step in the automatic linked sensori-motor response, conscious awareness allows us to determine whether we were correct in our prediction of what was seen, decided or done. If predictions prove inaccurate, consciousness allows us to shift out of 'automatic' into a 'choice about' perception, decision, action. You notice you have mis-spoken and make the correction.

According to Llinas, and Edelman as well, as long as inputs from the environment are consistent with predictions there is no need for consciousness! When actual inputs do not match with predictions, consciousness intervenes. Because it involves a high degree of integration between brain regions, consciousness allows for rapid selective choice between alternative responses. The banana you are reaching for has an unexpected colour and texture. Consciousness enables you to recognise it as a plastic fake, not worth picking up. Unless the environment changes in a way that is not anticipated, the brain just keeps doing what it has been doing. This is why you can keep driving without being consciously aware of the road, thinking of something else, until your exit appears.

Premotor-sensory connectivity is illustrated when research subjects wear inverted lenses for extended periods of time. Initially subjects 'see' the world as upside-down (inconsistently with vestibular and proprioceptive inputs). As subjects actively walk around, sensory activity is automatically adjusted. Subjects again 'see' the world right side up (consistently with other sensory inputs). Subjects who only passively experience the world (i.e. sitting on a chair with wheels) do not adapt to the inverted lenses. Llinas concludes that behavioural *interaction* with the environment modifies intrinsically generated images.

Coherence and cognitive binding

Brain modules process the individual stimulus features of the environment (for more on perception see Chapter 2). Currently the most accepted hypothesis for feature 'binding' and 'discrimination' is that neural cells responding to the same 'feature' develop a synchronous firing pattern. In binding features of a cup (i.e. contours, colour, texture) all cells responding to features of the cup exhibit synchronous firing patterns. In discriminating between two auditory tones, all cells responding to each frequency exhibit synchronous patterns of firing. The inferior olive, thalamus and neocortex have intrinsic activity that, Llinas theorises, functions as a 'pacemaker' to entrain the synchronous activity in widely distributed neural groups (Llinas, 1990; Llinas & Pare, 1996).

Llinas, as well as others, such as Crick (1994), theorise that in human beings 40 Hz oscillatory activity in the sensory cortex is particularly involved in conscious perception of stimuli. Subjects are presented with six sets of two clicks at inter-stimulus intervals from 3 to 30 milliseconds, and report whether they 'hear' one or two clicks. At intervals up to 13.7 msec only one click is consciously perceived. At intervals greater than 13.7, two clicks are consciously perceived. Magnetoencephalography (MEG) can be used to determine the presence or absence of 40 Hz activity in various cortical regions. MEG is a non-invasive technique that can localise cortical brain activity by means of surface (i.e. scalp) recordings of the underlying cerebral cortex. MEG recordings are selectively sensitive to the magnetic fields that arise from current flows in cortical neurons. MEG recordings over the auditory cortex reveal that

when two clicks are presented, but only one is consciously perceived, only one peak of synchronous firing at 40 Hz is observed.
When two clicks are presented, and two consciously perceived, two
peaks at 40 Hz are observed.

Except for smell, sensory messages from the world reach the
cortex through the thalamus and 'loop back' to the thalamus, via
thalamo-cortical neural circuits. The thalamo-cortical circuits are
divided into two looped systems, the specific and the intralaminar.
In the specific system, sensory information retains its modality
specificity, such as colour or sound frequency. In the intralaminar
circuits sensory information is diffuse, meaning that the modality
specificity of the sensory information is not identifiable. Both
'loops' make connections with the reticular nucleus of the thalamus. Llinas theorises that 40 Hz oscillatory activity in thalamo-
cortical circuits binds stimulus features into conscious spatio-
temporal events (Llinas, 1990, 1991; Llinas & Pare, 1996). Along
with Edelman and Tononi, he proposes that a 'conjunction of synchronous activity' between the specific and intralaminar loops,
made possible by connections in the reticular nucleus, produces
the binding necessary for consciousness. The content of consciousness is carried in the specific system and the temporal context in the intralaminar system. Together they generate a single
cognitive event. Damage to specific circuits leads to deficits only
in consciousness of individual sensory modalities. Damage to
intralaminar circuits leads to deep disturbances in consciousness.
Llinas believes the intralaminar nucleus of the thalamus serves as
a 'pacemaker' to synchronise activity at 40 Hz in modular brain
regions.

EDELMAN AND TONONI: NEURAL DARWINISM

Edelman and co-investigator Tononi are basically in agreement with many, although not all, of Llinas's ideas. They fundamentally agree that the brain is a closed system; that sensory and motor functions are automatically linked towards adaptive responses to the environment; that the thalamocortical system is central to consciousness; that consciousness is the result of synchronisation and binding together of diverse modular activity; and that there is no localised 'place' in the brain that co-ordinates and organises modular activity (Edelman, 1989, 1992; Tononi et al., 1992). The theoretical work of Edelman and Tononi is derived from Edelman's Nobel Prize-winning research, in which he discovered that the immune system operates along the same principles of population variation and selection that Darwin proposed for species evolution. Edelman (1998) believes that variation and selection in populations is a fundamental aspect of biological forms. His theoretical application of Darwin's theory to development and function of the higher vertebrate brain is called 'neural Darwinism' or the theory of neuronal group selection (TNGS).

Theory of neuronal group selection: variation, selection and re-entry

All neuroscientists agree that the function of the brain is to generate adaptive behavioural responses to the environment. The question they all face is 'could a programme of genetic instructions account for all the possible responses to environmental situations an animal is likely to encounter?' For life forms only capable of a few reflexive responses to a limited set of stimulus inputs (move towards light, withdraw from loud noises) a genetic programme might be sufficient. But in the case of the higher vertebrate brain, which is capable of perceiving such a variety of stimulus situations and responding in such flexible ways, most neuroscientists assume that the material contained in the genome is not enough. In essence, Edelman developed his model as a way of explaining both that no set of genetic instructions produces our ability to respond adaptively to the world and that while our experience is unified, there is no anatomical location where unity is accomplished.

TNGS hypothesises that the genome programmes only for the rough outlines of neurons and synapses. It goes on to speculate that the brain can develop all the necessary functional neural pathways it needs for adaptive behavioural responses, without specific genetic instructions, because of the specialised nature of its anatomy and physiology. The theory contains three basic points regarding this 'specialised nature' of the brain. The first is developmental selection. At birth, genetic programmes have laid out a general anatomical arrangement of neurons and synapses with an over-abundance of synaptic connections. An almost infinite 'variation' of ways exist for these neurons and synapses to be functionally organised into neural networks.

The second point is experiential selection. Overlapping the early post-natal period and continuing on throughout life, experience carves the functional neuronal pathways from the rough anatomical layout. The network pathways that are actually utilised during experience are selected by strengthening the synaptic connections between the neurons. Those not utilised are weakened and pruned back. By analogy, Manhattan has streets and intersections that result from a 'city plan'. The possible 'routes' people actually take to get home, to work, to school or to play are almost infinite and result from actual experience.

The third point is the process of re-entry. Re-entry refers to the idea that the brain contains massive parallel neural connections between brain regions that enable bi-directional reciprocal electrical signalling, such that activities in different modular regions mutually influence one another. Although re-entry is Edelman's term, most other neuroscientists would agree with the idea of massive parallel bi-directional signalling. Massive re-entry connections exist between the cortex, and structures such as the thalamus, basal ganglia, hippocampus and cerebellum. The amplification of synaptic transmission made possible through re-entry permits local neural activity to influence rapidly the selection of neural pathways linking even distant brain regions.

TNGS uses re-entry as the key mechanism for explaining how there is unity of perception and behaviour despite the fact that there is no 'central processor' or detailed set of instructions co-ordinating functionally segregated areas. Edelman and Tononi (Lumer et al., 1997) propose that the synchronisation of activity made possible by re-entry enables rapid shifts in activity in large populations of neuronal groups. Re-entry functions to 'select' the particular neural pathway that underlies the perceptual and behavioural experience of the animal by linking widely distributed areas into complicated patterns, rather than by feeding all the information into some centrally co-ordinating region. This is why consciousness takes time. Stimuli, memory or emotions must persist for sufficient duration to enable re-entry to produce the synchronisation of firing necessary to integrate widely distributed neural networks.

Complexity theory further refines the TNGS (Tononi et al., 1994). Consciousness requires the complexity inherent in the coexistence of localised segregation in conjunction with overall integration. In a process Edelman and Tononi refer to as *differentiation*, the modular activity that is integrated involves not only those neuronal groups that become active in the experience, but those that are inactive as well. What this means is that to be conscious of a particular sensory event, such as the colour red, is to simultaneously distinguish it as 'not yellow, not blue, even not sound and not touch'. Similarly Kinsbourne (1995) argues that what we are consciously aware of depends on its relation to other contents of which we are not consciously aware.

The value system

Despite enormous plasticity there are constraints on the eventual organisation of the brain. What is referred to by neuroscientists as the value system serves as a bias towards selecting those neural pathways that bring about behaviours that enhance survival. For example, as an infant develops the ability to grasp and eventually to feed itself, roughly speaking, two value constraints that are considered to operate are 'movement to midline is better than movement away from midline' and 'eating is better than not eating'. What this means is that in the early phase of the process a variety of pathways are activated, but eventually the synaptic connections are

strengthened in those neural pathways that subserve the value constraints. For example, a baby begins with random hand and arm
movements. It develops the ability to grasp an object held directly
in front of it, as the neural pathways that become active when the
baby moves its hand towards the midline are selectively strengthened over those neural pathways that are activated as the baby
flings its arm outwards. In order for grasping to become refined
into self-feeding, networks that subserve movements associated
with successfully getting food to the mouth are 'selected' over pathways subserving shaky movements that occasionally get food to the
infant's cheek. Most generally agree that value constraints are the
result of cholinergic and aminergic neuromodulatory systems,
since acetylcholine, dopamine, norepinephrine and serotonin neurotransmitters modulate changes in synaptic strength.

Experimental data in human beings support the idea that 'values'
such as motivational salience influence neural selective mechanisms.
Tachistoscopic presentation of a series of dots will not be perceived
consciously if the duration of each stimulus presentation is too short.
If the duration is lengthened to a few milliseconds, under normal conditions the subject will say, 'I see something but I don't know what'.
However, if the subject is deprived of food, they will say, 'I see pieces
of meat', and if deprived of water, they say, 'I see droplets of water'.

The hierarchy of brain functions that leads to consciousness

Objects in the outside world activate patterns of neural activity
in the brain. According to neuroscientists, perception involves the

brain's ability to recognise the patterns of neural activity not the objects themselves. These patterns result when re-entry correlates activity within multiple sensory modalities and the motivational value system. For example, a specific correlation of colour, contour and texture may lead to a neural pattern 'recognised' as apple but that is more likely to be perceived when the animal is hungry rather than satiated.

Edelman, perhaps more than other neuroscientists, emphasises the distinction between primary consciousness and self-reflective consciousness. According to Edelman primary consciousness is the awareness of the current perceptual scene in 'real time', i.e. the 'here and now'. It is produced when re-entry connections link ongoing perception with a special kind of memory referred to as value category memory. This is the conceptual memory of what has been salient in the animal's environment, essentially the animal's experiences of 'reward' and 'adversity'. Primary consciousness provides a coherent scene that allows the animal to link complex changes in the environment, which may not be causally associated in the outside world, but which help the animal to predict danger or reward. For example, value category memory stores the information 'this tree is near where I encountered a predator last time I was at the watering hole'. Even though the tree and predator are not 'causally linked in the environment' their association is salient and therefore they are meaningfully linked in value category memory and thus linked in an ongoing conscious scene.

What differentiates human beings from animals is the capacity for self-reflective consciousness (SRC). Primary consciousness exists only in 'current concrete' experience. Edelman's hypothesis is that SRC results from re-entry correlations of the 'present and concretely bound' primary consciousness with activity in symbolising and language regions such as prefrontal cortex, Broca's and Wernicke's regions. The prefrontal region symbolises experience that occurs during the social transmission of language. In this way, during verbal interactions with others, the brain generates symbolic categories such as self, non-self, actions, images, even its own internal sensations, and relates them to ongoing events of primary consciousness. Symbolic categorisation frees SRC from the constraints of the immediate present. The contents of SRC can be held in mind and manipulated without resorting to interaction with concrete aspects of the external world. In many ways Damasio's (1999) view of consciousness is quite similar to Edelman's, although Damasio has different terminology and a different emphasis. Edelman, coming from his Darwinian viewpoint, emphasises selection and the role of re-entry in integrating various brain systems. Damasio, coming from his emotion and 'somatic marker' hypothesis, emphasises the role of the body, the somatosensory cortex and brainstem nuclei during conscious experience.

Binocular rivalry

Binocular rivalry is one of the best ways to study the neural correlates of conscious awareness, because it illustrates how sensory inputs may impinge on the brain but not be consciously perceived. Edelman and Tononi (Tononi et al., 1998) use it to defend their idea that consciousness, rather than resembling a bright spotlight illuminating a small area on a dark stage, as many (such as Baars, 1996) conceptualise it, but involves high degrees of integrated activity between many regions of the brain, even the 'silent', 'dark' ones.

Rivalry occurs when two dissimilar images are presented to the two eyes. The individual consciously sees only one image at a time, with a switch in perceptual dominance occurring every few seconds. Perceptual transitions between each view occur spontaneously without any change in the physical stimulus. You can experience this phenomenon using the Necker cube (see Chapter 2, p. 28). Each eye observes a slightly different orientation of the cube. As one looks directly at the cube, the conscious perception spontaneously alternates between the two orientations. Binocular rivalry is one phenomenon used to distinguish between attentional mechanisms and conscious perception, since even though attention is directed at a constant image the subjective conscious perception fluctuates.

Neural responses associated with the physical presence of the stimulus can be distinguished from those associated with conscious awareness of the percept (Farber & Churchland, 1995). Rivalry studies in monkeys using single cell recording and in human beings using fMRI[1] indicate that activity reflecting the physical presence of the stimulus remains constant in 'striate' visual cortices (Lumer et al., 1998). However, when the stimulus is consciously perceived,

---

[1] Functional magnetic resonance imaging (fMRI) can detect changes in oxygen consumption. It can be used to measure localised neuronal activity in the brain because glucose is metabolised when neurons generate electrical impulses and oxygen consumption is a reflection of glucose metabolism. Like positron emission tomography (PET), which also measures glucose metabolism, fMRI has excellent localising ability; in addition it has significantly better temporal resolution.

activity in 'extrastriate' visual cortex and inferotemporal cortex shows alterations that correspond to each perception. Tononi et al. (1998) investigate binocular rivalry in human beings using MEG, which measures activity simultaneously in all cortical regions. With the use of special goggles, one eye is presented with the image of a red vertical grating and the other eye is presented with a blue horizontal grating. Both images are presented continuously, but subjects consciously perceive only one image at a time, with spontaneous alterations between the two. Brain activity for each stimulus is widely distributed throughout the cortex, whether or not the subject consciously perceives the stimulus. But the areas where activity is more intense differ according to whether the stimulus is perceived consciously or not. They conclude that this supports the idea that consciousness involves shifts in synchronous firing in large, distributed populations of neurons.

HOBSON: DREAMING AS A 'STATE' OF CONSCIOUSNESS

The dream research of Hobson is included in this discussion because it assumes many of the postulates of Llinas, Edelman and Tononi and serves as an illuminating application of their theoretical models. He assumes that the brain is essentially a closed system with intrinsically generated neural activity and the similarity in EEG activity indicates that dreaming and waking are alternate states of consciousness (Hobson, 1994; Hobson et al., 1998; Braun et al., 1998).

Hobson focuses on the three cardinal brain-mind states: waking, dreaming and non-dream sleeping. Numerous animal studies indicate that during the waking state the aminergic neuromodulatory systems (i.e. noradrenergic and serotonergic) are 'on' and the cholinergic system is dampened (Hobson et al., 1998). During REM sleep the opposite is the case, with the aminergic 'off' and the cholinergic 'on'. In other words, REM sleep is generated by the cholinergic system and waking by the aminergic system. Hobson's theory is that shifts between brain–mind states are produced by 'reciprocal interaction' of aminergic and cholinergic neuromodulatory systems. During waking, aminergic activation inhibits activity in cholinergic neurons and REM activity is suppressed. Reciprocally, during REM sleep, the aminergic system is 'turned off', releasing the cholinergic system and dream activity from suppression. What results is that waking consciousness is mediated by noradrenalin and serotonin, and dream consciousness by acetylcholine. Hobson's hypothesis is supported by a number of pharmacological studies. For example, noradrenergic agonists (clonidine) injected into the brainstem decrease REM. Reciprocally, cholinergic agonists and cholinesterase inhibitors (carbachol) induce REM sleep.

After studying literally thousands of human subjects who are awakened during different stages of sleep and asked to report their antecedent mental activity, what Hobson (and numerous others) have found is that, while dreams do occur during non-REM sleep, those that occur during REM sleep tend to be more bizarre and more vivid. Hobson has identified highly consistent characteristics that distinguish dream cognitions from waking ones. REM dreams are filled with strange associations between objects, scenes and actions. Orientation as to time, place, person and focus of attention are continually and rapidly shifting. Recent memory is patchy. Insight is almost absent. Emotions run high and involve mainly anxiety, anger and joy. From this perspective, dreaming is similar to an organic 'delirium', but in the case of dreaming it occurs nightly and we 'recover' each morning.

These aspects of dream cognition are presumed to reflect the differential activation of various brain regions resulting from the differential projections of the aminergic and cholinergic systems. These systems originate from a variety of nuclei in the pons and project widely to other brain regions. The cholinergic system originates from nuclei in the mesopontine tegmentum. PET scans during REM, when cholinergic circuits predominate, reveal that activity is increased in extrastriate visual cortex, basal ganglia, limbic and paralimbic regions, and activity in striate (i.e. primary) visual cortex and frontal cortex is decreased. Conversely in the waking state, PET scans reveal that striate and frontal cortex are activated. Hobson suggests that because of the almost seizure-like electrical firing that characterises REM sleep, pontine activation of limbic, basal ganglia and extrastriate visual areas causes dreams to contain highly disorganised, emotionally intense visuo-motor programmes. Since during REM the activity in primary sensory and frontal cortex is dampened, rational thought and sensori-motor responsivity to the external world is likewise diminished. Hobson agrees with the idea proposed by Llinas, Edelman and Tononi that dreams are a conscious brain state unmodified by external reality. The main difference between dreaming and waking is that, during REM dreaming, cortical regions that mediate interaction with the external world (primary sensory and frontal cortex) are shut down and information processing is driven instead by internal sources (pontine cholinergic circuits). The reason we can't orient ourselves in our dreams or remember them is that the aminergic systems that sustain orientation and memory are shut down. Hobson argues that dreams contain strange associations, not due to unconscious dynamics, but because sensori-motor cortices are driven by highly excitable centres in the pons without the top-down control of the 'rational' and 'volitional' frontal cortex. However they are emotionally meaningful because they include salient emotional memory contained in limbic circuits.

No conclusive answer has emerged regarding the function of either sleep in general or REM sleep in particular. Hobson believes that the most promising avenue of research implicates REM sleep as a means of consolidation of learning and memory. The aminergic neuromodulatory system that supports the acquisition of new information is shut down during REM, and therefore memory cannot be acquired. However, under the sway of the cholinergic system during REM, learning and memory consolidation occurs as synaptic strengthening forges new connections between the 'already acquired' information contained in the sensori-motor and emotional programmes of dream sleep. Although there is much debate on this issue, the work of Reiser (1991) is pertinent here. Reiser notes research showing the influence of the day residue on dream content, and points out that the apparently random aspects of dreaming stimulated by the pontine-geniculate-occipital (PGO) waves, actually favours themes resulting from recent activities, and leads to associations that can be psychodynamically significant.

CLINICAL CORRELATION AND CONCLUSIONS

For every evolutionary advance there is a price. The symbolic thinking embedded in self-reflective consciousness affords an almost infinite flexibility in the ways human beings can conceptualise the events of their life. The price is indecision. Too many possibilities as to how to interpret events lead to confusion over what behavioural response to choose. According to a theory of Ramachandran (Ramachandran et al., 1996), coherent belief systems evolved to narrow the number of choices in order to provide consistency and coherency in determining what to think and how to behave. Ramachandran uses the condition known as anosognosia to support his theory. Anosognosia manifests in the small percentage of patients with right-sided stroke who deny their illness (Bisiach & Berti, 1995; see also Chapter 5). When asked to perform a task, such as pointing to the doctor's nose with their left hand, patients deny their disability but come up with ingenious excuses as to why they cannot perform the task: 'I would like to, but I have terrible arthritis and it hurts too badly to lift my arm'.

Anosognosia has generally been considered a defence against the painful awareness of disability. Ramachandran argues that this explanation fails because patients with left-sided stroke, an equally upsetting disability, rarely display anosognosia. He argues instead that anosognosia results from the different role played by the right and left hemisphere with respect to belief systems. The left hemisphere is the interpreter, and is primarily concerned with taking all the bewildering sensory inputs and making sense of them by ordering them into a coherent belief system. By limiting the number of ways to interpret events, the brain is not overwhelmed by all the possible explanations that could be arrived at. This protects the brain from being paralysed by indecision as to how to act. The left hemisphere's goal is to maintain its belief system at all costs. When information inconsistent with the belief system occurs, rather than revise the belief system, the left hemisphere either denies the inconsistent information, or 'confabulates' to make it consistent. Thus we analyse the data in our sensory environment in terms of the belief systems we have constructed.

The strategy of the right hemisphere is fundamentally different. The right hemisphere functions as an anomaly detector. When inconsistent information reaches a sufficient threshold, the right hemisphere 'decides' it is time to revise the belief system. If, however, in the case of right-hemisphere stroke the anomaly detector function is impaired, the unimpaired left-sided interpreter maintains its original beliefs. Despite seeing that the left arm is paralysed, instead of revising the belief system (i.e. that the body is healthy), the left hemisphere denies the paralysis and confabulates to rationalise the motor incapacity. An experimental procedure as odd as the syndrome itself, suggests that the patient is consciously aware of the paralysis 'at some level'. Cold water is irrigated into the patient's left ear (right hemisphere). For a period of up to thirty minutes, the patient's denial clears and they acknowledge their disability. It seems as if the increased stimulation to the right hemisphere may temporarily repair the anomaly detector.

Gazzaniga (1998), who originated the concept of the left-hemisphere interpreter function, supports Ramachandran's theory of a differential cognitive role for right and left hemisphere that can lead to incorrect perceptions. In a test of memory with split-brain patients, when asked to report on an experience, the right brain reports a veridical account and the left generates many false reports. It is theorised that as a result of the left hemisphere always looking for the order and meaning of experience even when there is none, it can also include false information in its schema of what happened, if it fits with the belief. In a test of predictive capability, a subject must guess whether a light is going to appear at the top or bottom of a computer screen by pushing a button. The experimenter manipulates the situation so that 80 per cent of the time the stimulus appears on the top, but in a random sequence. It is quickly evident to all subjects that the light appears on top more often. Invariably, normal subjects adopt the strategy of trying to figure out the pattern and deeply believe that they can. However, using their strategy they are correct only 68 per cent of the time. If on the other hand, they had simply pushed the top button every time they would have been correct 80 per cent of the time! Rats, whose brain does not have the interpreter function, press only the top button and are correct more often than the normal human beings. Tests with split-brain patients reveals that the right brain appears to react in a way similar to the rat, responding most closely to what is there and not trying strategically to identify meaningful patterns.

Although the theories of Ramachandran (the right-hemisphere anomaly detector) and Gazzaniga (the left-hemisphere interpreter) are speculative, they suggest a number of clinically relevant points. Our conscious belief systems influence what we consciously perceive. The result is that conscious perceptions may not accurately reflect what occurs 'out there' in our environment. Additionally it implies that not only do people resist knowledge of unconscious mental contents, they resist knowledge of conscious material as well, if it does not fit with their consciously held interpretations of reality. What may occur during the interpretation of transference is the engagement of the anomaly detector in the right hemisphere, alerting the individual to the need to revise their neurotic belief system.

In conclusion, primary consciousness and self-reflective consciousness evolved to enhance survival. Presumably primitive organisms do not have consciousness. They respond with 'hardwired' inborn reflexive behaviour. Even in human beings, that which we do automatically, such as riding a bike or tying shoelaces, does not require conscious monitoring. Also, when no salient or meaningful change occurs in the environment, we do not attend consciously, as in the case of driving and not consciously paying attention. What consciousness provides is a means by which we notice changes and can flexibly choose the most adaptive response to that change. Consciousness provides a feedback system for the individual to monitor rapidly not only changes in the environment, but also their own minute-to-minute responses to those changes. We attend to and may be conscious of the most salient changes that occur.

In self-reflective consciousness, the self is taken as an object. Once the self can become an object of perception and interpersonal interactions can become internalised, one can reflect on one's own patterns of behaviour, and one can represent them symbolically. A representation of any sort is more malleable than that which it represents. At the level of human self-reflective consciousness we have 'representations of representations' that can be manipulated independently of 'concrete reality'. As a result of the flexibility inherent in consciousness we are open, on one hand, to forgetting and distortions, but on the other to the possibility of learning, growth and therapeutic change.

REFERENCES

BAARS, B. (1996). *In the Theater of Consciousness: The Workspace of the Mind.* New York: Oxford Univ. Press.

BISIACH, E. & BERTI, A. (1995). Consciousness in dyschiria. In *The Cognitive Neurosciences.* Cambridge, MA: MIT Press, pp. 1331–1340.

BRAUN, A. R. ET AL. (1998). Dissociated pattern of activity in visual cortices and their projection during human rapid eye movement sleep. *Science,* 279: 91–94.

CHALMERS, D. (1996). *The Conscious Mind: In Search of a Fundamental Theory.* Oxford: Oxford Univ. Press.

CHURCHLAND, P. S. (1996). *Toward a Neurobiology of the Mind. The Mind-Brain Continuum.* Cambridge, MA: MIT Press, pp. 281–303.

CRICK, F. (1994). *The Astonishing Hypothesis.* New York: MacMillan.

DAMASIO, A. R. (1999). *The Feeling of What Happens.* New York: Harcourt Brace and Co.

—— & DAMASIO, H. (1996). Making images and creating subjectivity. In *The Mind-Brain Continuum.* Cambridge, MA: MIT Press, pp. 19–27.

DEACON, T. W. (1997). *The Symbolic Species.* New York: W. W. Norton.

DENNETT, D. C. (1991). *Consciousness Explained.* Canada: Little, Brown & Co. Ltd.

ECCLES, J. C. (1989). *Evolution of the Brain: Creation of the Self.* New York: Routledge.

EDELMAN, G. (1989). *The Remembered Present.* New York: Basic Books.

—— (1992). *Bright Air, Brilliant Fire.* New York: Basic Books.

—— (1998). Building a picture of the brain. *Daedalus,* 127: 37–69.

—— & TONONI, G. (2000). *A Universe of Consciousness.* New York: Basic Books.

FARBER, I. B. & CHURCHLAND, P. S. (1995). Consciousness and the neurosciences: philosophical and theoretical issues. In *The Cognitive Neurosciences.* Cambridge, MA: MIT Press, pp. 1295–1306.

GAZZANIGA, M. S. (1998). The split brain revisited. *Scientific American,* July issue: 50–55.

—— ET AL. (1962). Some functional effects of sectioning the cerebral commisures in man. *Proc. Nat. Acad. Sci. USA,* 48: 1765–1769.

GRAY, J. (1995). The contents of consciousness: a neuropsychological conjecture. *Behav. & Brain Sci.,* 18: 659–722.

HIRST, W. (1995). Cognitive aspects of consciousness. In *The Cognitive Neurosciences.* Cambridge, MA: MIT Press, pp. 1307–1319.

HOBSON, J. A. (1994). *The Chemistry of Conscious States.* Boston: Little, Brown & Co.

—— ET AL. (1998). The neuropsychology of REM sleep dreaming. *NeuroReport,* 9: R1–R14.

HUMPHREY, N. (1992). *A History of the Mind.* London: Chatto & Windus.

KINSBOURNE, M. (1995). Models of consciousness: serial or parallel in the brain? In *The Cognitive Neurosciences.* Cambridge, MA: MIT Press, pp. 1321–1329.

—— (1998). Unity and diversity in the human brain. *Daedalus*, 127: 233–256.

KNIGHT, R. T. & GRABOWECKY, M. (1995). Escape from linear time: prefrontal cortex and conscious experience. In *The Cognitive Neurosciences*. Cambridge, MA: MIT Press, pp. 1357–1371.

LAKOFF, G. & JOHNSON, M. (1980). *Metaphors We Live By*. Chicago, IL: Univ. Chicago Press.

LIBET, B. ET AL. (1983). Time of conscious intention to act in relation to onset of cerebral activity (readiness potential): the unconscious initiation of a freely voluntary act. *Brain*, 106: 623–642.

LLINAS, R. R. (1990). Intrinsic electrical properties of mammalian neurons and CNS function. *Fidia Research Foundation Neuroscience Award Lectures*, 4: 175–194.

—— & CHURCHLAND, P. S. (EDS) (1996). *The Mind-Brain Continuum*. Cambridge, MA: MIT Press.

—— & PARE, D. (1996). The brain as a closed system modulated by the senses. In *The Mind–Brain Continuum*, ed. R. Llinas & P. Churchland. Cambridge, MA: MIT Press, pp. 1–18.

LUMER, E. D. ET AL. (1997). Neural dynamics in a model of the thalamocortical system. II. The role of neural synchrony tested through perturbations of spike timing. *Cerebral Cortex*, 7: 228–236.

—— (1998). Neural correlates of perceptual rivalry in the human brain. *Science*, 280: 1930–1934.

MOSCOVITCH, M. (1995). Models of consciousness and memory. In *The Cognitive Neurosciences*. Cambridge, MA: MIT Press, pp. 1341–1356.

MOUNTCASTLE, V. B. (1998). Brain science at the century's ebb. *Daedalus*, 127: 1–36.

OLDS, D. D. (1990). Brain-centered psychology: a semiotic approach. *Psychoanal. Contemp. Thought*, 13: 331–363.

—— (1992). Consciousness: a brain-centered informational approach. *Psychoanal. Inq.*, 12: 419–444.

—— (1995). A semiotic model of mind. Presented at American Psychoanalytic Association Meeting, December 1995.

PENROSE, R. (1994). *Shadows of the Mind.* Oxford: Oxford Univ. Press.

PINKER, S. (1997). *How the Mind Works.* New York: W. W. Norton.

RAMACHANDRAN, V. S. ET AL. (1996). Illusions of body image: what they reveal about human nature. In *The Mind–Brain Continuum.* Cambridge, MA: MIT Press, pp. 29–60.

REISER, M. F. (1991). *Memory in Mind and Brain.* New York: Basic Books.

SEARLE, J. R. (1997). *The Mystery of Consciousness.* New York: New York Review of Books.

SHEVRIN, H. ET AL. (1996). *Conscious and Unconscious Process: Psychodynamic, Cognitive, and Neuropsychological Convergence.* New York: Guilford Press.

SOLMS, M. (1997). What is consciousness? *J. Amer. Psychoanal. Assn.*, 45: 681–778.

TONONI, G. ET AL. (1992). Reentry and the problem of integrating multiple cortical areas: simulation of dynamic integration in the visual system. *Cerebral Cortex*, 2: 310–335.

—— ET AL. (1994). A measure for brain complexity: relating functional segregation and integration in the nervous system. *Proc. Nat. Acad. Sci.*, 91: 5033–5037.

—— ET AL. (1998). Investigating neural correlates of conscious perception by frequency-tagged neuromagnetic responses. *Neurobiol.*, 95: 3198–3203.

WEISER, T. N. & HUBEL, D. H. (1974). Ordered arrangement of orientation columns in monkeys lacking visual experience. *J. Comp. Neurol.*, 158: 307–318.

INDEX

Activity levels, and perception, 32

Adolphs, 112

Affect. *See* Emotion

Agha, A., 119

Alkon, D., 43

Aminergic neuromodulatory system, 165, 170–171, 172

Amygdala
and memory, 52, 59–62, 63
appraisal of stimuli in, 76–77, 80
development of, 88
effects of separation on, 94
in emotional arousal, 85, 125
in fear and anxiety reactions, 82–83, 85–88
in non-verbal communication, 97

Anosognosia
and levels of consciousness, 144
as result of right parietal lobe damage, 111–112, 149
on choice of behaviours, 173–174

Anxiety disorders, 85–88

Aphasia, 105, 109, 116–117

Art, right hemisphere dominance in, 109–110

Association cortices, and levels of consciousness, 144

Attachment, emotional, 15, 92–95, 128

Attention
and perception, 32–33, 38–39
distraction of, 91–92
effects of emotional arousal on, 89–90
in consciousness, 145–146, 147, 176

Auditory cortex
in conditioned fear reaction, 82–83
in language, 116

Autonomic nervous system
effects of emotions on, 89, 90–91, 98
in emotional processing, 61, 77–78, 127
response to empathic attunement, 97
response to imagined emotions, 96
right hemisphere dominance in, 108

Avoidance, and conditioned fear reaction, 84

Baars, B., 147

Baddeley, A., 43, 45, 46

Bailey, C. H., 11

Barinaga, M., 21, 25, 32
Basal ganglia, 163, 171
    in memory, 58–59, 61–62
    motor patterns stored in, 3–4
Beardsley, R., 31, 46
Bechara, A., 60, 83, 98–99
Beebe, B., 96–97
Behaviour, 4, 121, 163
    and perception, 35–36
    choice of, 85, 173–174, 176
    genetic basis for, 161–162
    influence of emotions on, 73, 75
    influences on, 13–14, 97
    musculo-skeletal in emotional
        processing, 77–79
    role of neural circuits in, 6–7
    stored motor patterns for, 3–4,
        157–158
Belief systems, left vs. right
        hemisphere in, 173–176
Berti, A., 144, 173
Bilaterality
    and schizophrenia, 128–129
    hemispheric specialisation,
        105–135
    in control of emotions, 126–
        128
Binding problem, 141–142, 159–
    160
Binocular rivalry, 167–169
Bisiach, E., 144, 173
Biver, F., 90
Blindsight, 148
Bloom, P., 117–118
Body image, 110, 111
Body, and duality of mind, 138–
    139. See also Brain

Bottom up processing, in
    perception, 23–29
Brain
    as closed system, 155–156, 169
    as reality emulator, 154–160
    capacity of, 3
    cellular architecture of, 2–3
    construction of perceptions by,
        19–39
    effects of emotional arousal on,
        89
    evolution of, 3–4
    plasticity of, 14–15, 155–156
    structures for explicit memory,
        49
    unconscious circuitry of, 74
Brain damage
    and schizophrenia, 128–129
    anosognosia and hemineglect
        from, 144
    aphasia from, 105, 109
    effects on consciousness, 150,
        160
    effects on language, 115–117
    effects on memory, 49, 56–59
    right hemisphere, 110–112
Brain development, influences on,
    4–13
Brain functions, 7
    hierarchy of, 165–167
    in perception, 20–25, 29–30,
        35–36
    integration of, 4, 150, 168
    responses to environment, 26–
        29, 161
    speed of, 35–36, 137
    the binding problem in, 141–142

Brain regions
  and bilaterality, 128–129
  connections between, 7–8, 13–
    14, 23–29, 34–35, 107, 115
  cortical and subcortical
    functions, 106
  development of hemispheres,
    114, 124–126
  disconnections between
    hemispheres, 64, 65, 131
  for consciousness, 79, 148–150
  for emotion, 82, 126–128
  for language, 115–116, 119–120
  for memory, 49–51
  for perception, 159
  hemispheric specialisation,
    105–135
  in belief systems, 173–174
  integration of hemispheres,
    105–107, 130
  left hemisphere, 64, 112–120
  neuromodulatory systems in, 171
  right hemisphere functions,
    108–112, 118
    language processing, 118–119
  self system in, 146
  split-brain studies of, 120–124
Brainstem, in emotional
  processing, 77–78
Braun, A. R., 169
Bremner, J. D., 62, 84, 87
Broca's area, 116–117
Broca, 105
Brothers, L., 22, 97

Cahill, L., 52
Calvert, C. A., 26

Calvin, W. H., 22, 23, 26, 32, 59,
  113
Caretakers, 91, 92–95, 154. *See
  also* Mothers
Cataracts, 8
Cerebellum, re-entry circuits to
  cortex, 163
Chalmers, D., 140, 142, 150
Character, 59. *See also*
  Temperament
Chen, M., 11
Chiron, C., 114, 124
Cholinergic neuromodulatory
  system, 165, 170–172
Churchland, P. S., 139, 140–141,
  145, 150, 168
Claparède, E., 74
Cognition, 58, 89
  brain regions associated with,
    126, 173–175
  dreaming *vs.* waking, 170–171
  in closed system model, 155–
    156
  organized by emotions, 73
  role of neural circuits in, 6–7
  use of long-term memory and
    working memory in, 46–47
Comparator, as model of
  consciousness, 146–147
Complexity theory, 164
Computers, and models of neural
  circuits, 6
Conditioned fear, 80–86
Conrad, A. S., 5
Consciousness, 44
  and "dual mind," 105–106,
    138–142

Consciousness (*continued*)
 and memory, 48–49, 52–53,
  62, 85
 and perception, 168–169
 as feedback system, 157–158
 content *vs.* process of, 147
 development of, 154, 176
 effects of trauma on, 64, 85
 effects on perception, 38–39
 emotions in, 79, 83
 function of, 150–154
 hierarchy of brain functions
  for, 165–167
 in split brain studies, 122–123
 in systems for perceptual
  speed *vs.* accuracy, 36, 39
 levels/states of, 143–144,
  169–172
 location of, 148–150
 nature of, 142–145, 150, 167–168
 neuroscience of, 137–177
 process of, 145–148, 163–164, 169
Context, right hemisphere
  dominance in, 108–110
Continuation, in grouping
  responses to stimulus, 28
Cooper, A., 1
Cooper, L. A., 34
Corbetta, M. F., 32
Corodimas, K. P., 85
Corpus callosum, 115, 120
Cortex, 4, 163. *See also*
  Orbitofrontal cortex; Prefrontal cortex; Sensory cortex
 in conditioned fear reaction,
  82–83
 in processing perceptions, 23–29

Crick Koch, 27
Crick, F., 19, 21, 24, 25, 27, 141–
  142, 159

Damasio, A. R., 4, 74, 111
 on consciousness, 167
 on emotions, 76, 98–99
 on self system, 146
Damasio, H., 146
Darwin, C., 73
Davidson, R. J., 127
Davis, M., 81, 86, 94
Dawson, G., 126–128, 130
De Yoe, E. A., 21
Deacon, T. W., 106, 117, 118–
  119, 153
Decartes, R., 138–139
Decision making
 consciousness of, 151–152
 influence of emotions on, 98–
  99
Declarative memory. *See* Explicit
  memory
Degangi, G. A., 91
Denial, in anosognosia, 111–112
Dennett, D. C., 139
Depression, effects on brain
  activity, 89–90
Desimone, R., 32
Development, 162
 environmental stimulation in,
  8–13
 of brain hemispheres, 124–126,
  132
 of consciousness, 154
 of hippocampus *vs.* amygdala,
  88

of language, 113–120
of memory, 61–62
plasticity *vs.* permanence of
    neural circuits in, 14–15,
    155–156
value system in selection of
    neural circuits, 164–165
Diamond, M. C., 7, 10–11, 15
Dissociation, in memory of
    trauma, 63–64
Dopaminergic circuits, 125, 129
Dreams, 156
as state of consciousness, 169–
    172
Drugs, effects on memory, 52

Eccles, J. C., 140
Edelman, G. M., 146, 158
neural Darwinism of, 160–169
on brain activity, 2–3, 4, 23,
    155
on consciousness, 19, 145, 148,
    150, 161
on perception, 6–8, 30, 38, 160
Ekman, P., 78–79, 95–96
Emotion, 14, 74
and brain hemispheres, 108–
    112, 121–122, 130–132
and language, 114, 130
and non-verbal
    communication, 95–98
and psychosomatic conditions,
    88–90
brain regions associated with,
    4, 6–7, 9–10, 126–128
cause and effect with
    behaviours, 75

development of, 9–10
effects on memory, 53, 55, 62–
    63
in brain's construction of
    perceptions, 19–20
in dreams, 172
in non-verbal communication,
    97
in therapy, 100, 130
influence of, 98
perception of social signals of,
    22
regulation of, 10, 84, 90–92,
    97–98, 124–126
survival purposes of, 73–74
terminology for, 79–80
Emotional memory, 59–61
Emotional processing, 31, 76–
    98
Empathic attunement, 96–97
Endocrine system, in emotional
    processing, 77–78
Engel, A. K., 27
Environment, 25
and brain development, 5–13
in perception, 19–39
prediction of, 156–158
Evolution
and brain in closed system
    model, 155–156
cost of emotional processing,
    88
function of consciousness in,
    150–152
of consciousness, 176–177
of emotion, 73
of fear, 80, 87

Evolution (*continued*)
  of speech, 117
  of speed *vs.* flexibility in brain
    functions, 137
  selection for survival
    behaviours in, 164–165
Experience, 31, 118
  effect on perception, 19
  effects on neural circuits, 6–7,
    162–163
  effects on perception, 29–30,
    36–38
  role in psychological
    functioning, 1–2
Explicit memory, 48–55, 61–63,
  149

False memory, 65–67, 154
Fantasy *vs.* reality, 34, 52
Farber, I. B., 168
Fear
  and anxiety disorders,
    85–88
  and memory, 60, 64
  conditioned, 80–86
Feldstein, S., 96
Fernald, A., 109
Fine motor control, left
    hemisphere dominance in,
    112–113
Finkel, L. F., 28
Fischer, K. W., 126–128,
  130
Flashbacks, 63
Fox, N. A., 127
Freedman, N., 97
Fried, I., 22

Frontal cortex
  activity in REM sleep, 171–172
  effects of emotional arousal on,
    89
Frontal lobe, effects of damage,
  110–111
Fuster, J. M., 4, 46

Galin, D., 106
Gazzaniga, M. S., 19
  on brain hemispheres, 105,
    109, 174–175
  on brain integration, 106
  split brain studies of, 120–123,
    148–149
Genetics, influence on brain
    development, 4–5
Gestalt criteria, for grouping
    responses to stimulus,
    28–29
Gilbert, C. D., 25
Gray, C. M., 27
Gray, J., 146, 150
Graziano, M. S., 35
Gregory, T. L., 25
Grigsby, J., 59
Gross, J. J., 97
Grossberg, S., 6
Gunnar, M., 90

Habituation, neuronal growth
    and learning, 11–12
Hadley, J., 6
Halgren, E., 83
Handedness, left hemisphere
    dominance in, 113
Hartlaub, G. H., 59

Hawkins, R. D., 11
Hebb's rule, 7
Hebb, D. O., 7
Hemineglect, 111, 144, 149
Henry, J. P., 90, 132
Hippocampus, 163
    and anxiety attacks, 86–87
    as centre for consciousness,
        149
    development of, 12–13, 88
    effects of emotional arousal on,
        62, 89
    in conditioned fear reaction,
        84–85
    in false memory, 65–67
    involvement in memory, 49–
        51, 52, 58, 60–62
Hirst, W., 143, 148
Hobson, J. A., 138, 145, 155,
    169–172
Hofer, M. A., 13, 92–93
Hormonal systems
    effects of stress on, 132
    in attachment, 94–95
Hubel, D. H., 9, 155
Hughlings-Jackson, 105
Humphrey, N., 152
Hypothalamus, 77–78, 84, 94
Hysteria, implicit and explicit
    memory in, 64

Iconic memory, 45
Imagery, 33–34
Imitation, and motor actions'
    relation to visual imagery, 34
Implicit learning, low-level
    analysis in, 143

Implicit memory, 55–63
Infants, 109
    attachment of, 92–95
    regulation of emotional arousal
        in, 90–91
    relations with mothers, 13–14,
        57, 96
Inferior parietal lobule (IPL),
    115–117, 126
Information processing, 106,
    112–113, 120–124
Insel, T., 94–95

Jacobs, T., 95
Jacobs, W. J., 86, 88
James, W., 75
Johnson, M., 147
Joseph, R., 106, 123
    on emotional processing, 76,
        84
    on hemispheric dominance,
        108, 109, 113
    on language development, 114,
        115
    on memory, 50, 54, 61
    on repression, 64, 131–132

Kalin, N. H., 14, 92, 94
Kandel, E. R., 11, 129
Kaniza triangle, 24, 156
Kaplan, J. A., 110–111
Kapp, B. S., 78
Kapur, S., 52
Kempermann, G., 12
Kendon, A., 98
Kinney, H. C., 5
Kinsbourne, M., 150, 156, 164

Knowlton, B. J., 48, 59
Koch, C., 27
Koenig, O., 34
Kosslyn, S. M., 30, 33, 34
  on encoding into memory, 52
Krasnegor, N., 85, 89, 91
Kupferman, I., 45, 48

La Bar, K. S., 83
Lachmann, F. M., 96–97
Lakoff, G., 147
Lange, 105
Language, 98, 167
  and emotion, 127–128, 130,
    131–132
  and hemispheric specialisation,
    105, 107, 113–120, 127–
    128
  and memory, 62, 64–65
  development of, 155–156
  effects of right frontal lobe
    damage on, 110–111
  in split brain studies, 120–124
  right hemisphere dominance
    in, 108
Lavender, J., 97
Le Vay S., 21
Learning, 143, 172
  and memory, 43, 58–60
  and neuronal growth, 11–12
  generalisation of, 88
  in psychoanalysis, 129
Learning disabilities, and left
    hemisphere development,
    115
LeDoux, J., 35, 59–61, 73
  on conditioned fear, 80, 82, 84

on emotional arousal, 84, 86–
    87, 89
  on emotional processing, 76
Left hemisphere. See Brain
    regions
Levin, F., 132
Libet, B., 150, 151
Limbic structures, 108, 114
  in emotional self-regulation,
    125–126
  in REM sleep, 171–172
Linear sequencing, left
    hemisphere dominance in,
    112–113
Llinas, R. R., 138
  on consciousness, 145, 148,
    150
  reality emulator model of, 154–
    160
Location, in conditioned fear
    reaction, 84
Locus coeruleus, activated in
    consciousness, 145
Long-term memory, 46–61
Lumer, E. D., 163, 168
Luria, A., 109

Maclean, P. D., 3
Maher, L. M., 116
McClelland, J. L., 33
McEwen, B. S., 62
McGaugh, J. L., 52, 62
Meltzoff, A. N., 114
Memory, 43–67
  and emotions, 73, 74, 89
  and hippocampus, 12–13, 85,
    149

brain regions associated with, 4, 8
disconnection of implicit and explicit, 61–62, 64
in container model of consciousness, 147
in perception, 20, 30–31
influences on, 156
information flow in, 44, 45–48
mechanisms of, 6–7, 52–55, 153–154, 172
types of, 43–48, 55–61, 166
Metaphors, for treating emotional disconnection, 132
Miller, E. K., 46, 113
Milner, B., 51
Mind, conceptualizations of, 138–139
Mind-brain relationship, 137–138, 140–141
Mishkin, M., 49
Modell, A., 132
Moran, J., 32
Moreno, C. R., 108
Moscovitch, M., 143, 149
Moskowitz, M., 48, 50, 55
Mothers, 154
   effects on brains of infants, 13–14
   empathic attunement with infants, 96
   in development of emotional self-regulation, 10, 91, 125–126
   infants' attachment to, 92–95

Motivation, in perception, 19–20, 31
Motor actions
   consciousness of, 150
   in sensori-motor templates, 157
   relation to visual imagery, 34–35
Motor skills
   for hand and mouth movements, 117
   in procedural memory, 58
   left hemisphere dominance in, 112–113
Mountcastle, V. B., 142
Music, right hemisphere dominance in, 109

Nadel, L.
   on explicit memory, 48, 49, 50
   on fear and anxiety reactions, 84, 86, 88
   on memory, 55, 58
Necker cube, 28, 29, 168
Neiser, U., 49
Nelson, K., 62
Neural circuits, 6–7, 145
   and learning, 11–12
   as sensori-motor templates, 157
   development of, 8–10, 12–13, 162
   information encoded in, 137–138
   plasticity vs. permanence of, 14–15, 155–156
   value system in selection of, 164–165

Neural Darwinism, 160–169

Neuromodulatory systems, 155–156, 170–171

Neurons
in visual processing hierarchy, 21–25
responses to different features of stimulus, 26–29

Neuroscience, relation to psychoanalysis, 1

Neuroses, and fear, 88

Non-verbal processes, 130
and emotion, 92, 95–98
brain regions for, 108–109, 126

Noradrenergic circuits, in emotional self-regulation, 125

O'Keefe, J., 49, 84

Object permanence, 35

Olds, D., 1, 141, 153

Optical illusions, 20, 24, 156

Orbitofrontal cortex
and emotions, 98–99, 124–126
appraisal of stimuli in, 76–77
in non-verbal communication, 97

Ornstein, R., 30, 105, 106, 107, 119, 120

Pally, R., 99

Panic states, development of, 87

Pare, D., 154–160

Parietal lobe, right, 110, 111, 149

Pattern matching, 6–7
in memory, 30–31
in perception, 19, 29–30, 37–39, 165–166

Penrose, R., 139–140

Perception, 6–7, 73, 156, 157
and attention, 145–146
and memory, 45, 52
brain regions for, 8, 109–110
brain's active construction of, 19–39
effects of binocular rivalry, 168–169
in closed system model, 155–156
integration of, 4, 150, 159–160, 163
internal vs. external, 147–148, 175–177
low-level analysis in, 143–144, 148
processing hierarchy in, 20–25
recognition of patterns in, 165–166
speed vs. accuracy in, 35–36, 39

Pfluger, M., 108

Phillips, R. G., 84

Philosophy, on consciousness, 138–139

Phobias, and evolution of 'prepared fears,' 87

Physiology, 73–74, 95
effects of infants' attachment on, 92–93
effects of separation on, 93–94
influence of non-verbal communication on, 99
of fear and anxiety reactions, 85–87
of psychosomatic conditions, 88–90

Pinker, S., 73, 117–118
Polymodal sensory information, 25
Porges, S. W., 90–91
Post-traumatic stress disorder, 62–63
Posterior cortex, effects of emotional arousal on, 89
Precortical structures, and vocalisation, 114
Prefrontal cortex, 59, 151
   development of, 9–10, 124–126
   functions of, 124
   in emotional self-regulation, 126
   in fear and anxiety reactions, 80, 83, 85
   in memory, 46, 51, 52, 61–62
   in REM sleep, 171–172
   symbolisation and language in, 167
Primary consciousness, 166–167, 176
Primed memory, 55–57, 143
Procedural memory, 58–59
Protein, to increase brain function, 11
Proximity, in grouping responses to stimulus, 28
Psychic reality, 156
Psychoanalysis
   and levels of consciousness, 144
   and memory research, 61
   as focused attention, 39
   comparator model of consciousness in, 146–147
      implication of integration of brain hemispheres, 130
      memory retrieval during, 54, 55
      non-verbal communication in, 99–100
      relation to neuroscience, 1
      results of, 15, 63, 129, 154
Psychosomatic conditions, 88–90

Ramachandran, V. S., 25, 173–174
Ramachandran, W. S., 111
Rao, S. C., 22
Re-entry circuits, 7–8, 23, 163–164, 166–167
Reality, vs. fantasy, 34, 52
Recognition, role of neural circuits in, 6–7
Redundancy, of neural circuits, 6–7
Reflexes, 150–151
Reiman, E. M., 76
Reiser, M. F., 172
Relationships. See also Social interactions
   empathic attunement in, 96–97
   hypothalamus in, 94–95
   separation in, 93–94
Repetition, effects of pattern matching on, 38
Repression, 44
   and false memory, 65–66
   due to disconnection between hemispheres, 131–132
   effects on memory, 48, 64

Retrieval, of memories, 53–55, 65–66
Right frontal lobe, in repression, 64
Right hemisphere. *See* Brain regions, right hemisphere
Risse, G. L., 122
Rizzolatti, O., 35
Rotenberg, V. S., 128–129
Rumelhart, D. E., 33

Sajda, P., 28
Sapolsky, R. M., 85, 87, 89
Schacter, D. L., 43, 44
  on explicit memory, 48, 50, 51
  on false memory, 66
  on memories of trauma, 63–64
  on types of memory, 56, 58, 61
Scheibel, A. B., 5, 114
Schizophrenia, 5, 128–129
Schore, A. N., 9–10, 15, 92, 97
  on emotional processing, 78, 124–125
  on hemispheric control of emotion, 108, 127
Searle, J. R., 139–141
Self system, in consciousness, 146
Self, as object of perception, 176–177
Self-reflection, 173
  as function of consciousness, 152, 166–167
  as trait of humans, 166–167
  evolution of, 176–177
Self-regulation, emotional, 130
  development of, 10, 124–126
  effects of mothers on, 13–14

Sensitisation, and learning, 11–12
Sensitive periods, of brain development, 8–10
Sensori-motor system, 156–158
Sensory context, in perception, 25
Sensory cortex, 171
  in false memory, 66–67
  in perception, 159–160
  need for stimulation of, 8–9
Sensory information, encoded in memory, 50–51
Sensory modalities, 25–26
Separation/reunion
  and attachment, 92–93
  and frontal lobe asymmetry, 126, 128
  effects on infants' brains, 13–14
Shepard, R. H., 34
Shevrin, H., 143
Shimamura, A. P., 43, 50
Siegel, D. J., 33, 62
Similarity, in grouping responses to stimulus, 28–29
Singer, W., 26, 27, 28
Sleep
  and dreams, 156, 169–172
  as state of consciousness, 145, 169–172
Social interactions, 73
  non-verbal communication in, 97
  perception of signals in, 22
  right hemisphere dominance in processing, 108–111
Solms, M., 147–148

Somaesthetic sensation
   in split brain studies, 122–123
   right hemisphere dominance
      in, 110–111
Speech. *See* Language
Spence, S., 127
Sperry, 105, 120–123
Split-brain patients, 120–124,
      148–149, 152, 175
Squire, L. R.
   on explicit memory, 48, 49, 50
   on types of memory, 55, 57,
      58
Stern, D., 10
Stimulation, need for, 8–9
Stimuli
   appraisal of, 26–29, 76–77
   attention to, 32, 89–90
   conscious perception of, 159–
      160
   effects of emotions on, 73, 89–
      90
   in fear reactions, 80, 82–83, 86
   in unconscious and
      consciousness, 143
Stress
   effects on memory, 52, 85
   emotional response to, 90
   increased likelihood of anxiety
      attacks due to, 86–87
Stress hormones, 52
Subliminal presentation, low-
      level analysis of, 143
Sussman, A. L., 30, 33, 34
Svensson, T. H., 87, 90
Symbolisation, linked with
      primary consciousness, 167

Temperament, 91, 128
Temporal sequencing, 112–113,
   118
Temporal sychronisation, 26–29,
   159, 163–164
Testosterone, effect on language
      development, 115
Thalamocortical neural circuits,
   160, 161
Thalamus, 160, 163
Theory of neuronal group
      selection (TNGS). *See*
      Neural Darwinism
Therapy. *See also* Psychoanalysis
   for emotional disconnection
      between hemispheres,
      132
Thinking. *See* Cognition
Thompson, D. M., 53
TNGS. *See* neural Darwinism
Tomkins, S., 97
Tononi, G., 3, 155
   on consciousness, 150, 161
   on neural Darwinism, 160–
      169
   on perception, 160, 169
Top down processing, in
      perception, 30–34
Transference, 31, 39, 176
Trauma, 33
   and false memory, 65–67
   effects of, 62–63, 83, 84
   repression of, 123, 131–132
Troise, A., 97–98
Tucker, D. M., 106, 108, 126
Tulving, E., 43, 44, 52, 53
Turnbull, O. H., 111

Unconscious, 85, 95
  and "dual mind," 138–142
  and fear reactions, 82, 86–87
  in neuroscience *vs.*
    psychoanalysis, 74
  relation to consciousness, 44,
    143

Value category memory, 166
Van der Kolk, B. A., 31
Van Essen, D. C., 21
Vargha-Khadem, F., 51
Vision
  and consciousness of objects,
    148–149
  binocular rivalry, 168–169
  in split brain studies, 120–124
  need for stimulation of sensory
    cortex, 8–9
  processing hierarchy in, 21–25

Visual cortex, 171
  and binocular rivalry, 168–169
  in processing hierarchy, 21–25
  relation to motor actions, 34–
    35
  stimulated by imagining, 33–34

Wada Test, 122–123, 131
Warrington, E. K., 46
Weisel, T. N., 155
Welkowitz, J., 96
Wernicke's area, 115–117
Wernicke, on aphasia, 105
Wickelgren, I., 46
Wiesel, T. N., 9
Wittling, W., 108
Working memory, 45–47

Zeki, S., 21
Zola-Morgan, S., 49, 50